Small Business Sales How-to Series
Book #2

Selling

101

Consultative Selling Skills

Michael McGaulley

ASIN: B003UNKZAO

ISBN-13: 978-0976840664

101-3-11-18 B

Published by Champlain House Media.   101 –P 1.1 21418

Printed in the United States

This publication is designed to provide accurate and authoritative information with regard to the subject matter covered. It is sold with the understanding that neither the author nor publisher is engaged in rendering legal, accounting, or other professional advice.

http://salestrainingsource.com/

PART ONE: LOCATING PRIORITY PROSPECTS

No matter how unique and innovative your product or service is, you can't effectively sell it to the whole world -- at least not at the start. Your time and energy, as well as your working capital, are limited. Don't spread them too thinly.

Therefore, begin by narrowing in on the best groups of prospects, and target your efforts especially on them. It's a rule-of-thumb in marketing that 80% of your sales (and profits) will come from 20% of your customers. By finding and focusing early on those high-payoff prospects, you greatly increase your chances of surviving . . . and ultimately succeeding.

Those in this primary target market are individuals or organizations that have a particularly strong need for what you offer, have the money, and that can be reached efficiently.

Others outside the target group may find their way to you and buy: that's fine. You won't turn them away, of course. But on the other hand you can't afford to waste effort on the lost cause of trying to find these improbables.

Naturally, the composition of the target markets may change or expand over time as conditions change, or as your awareness of your best markets grows. But at the start, you need to have definite prospect groups in mind, since precisely who these high-probability buyers are will likely influence the strategy and approach you evolve.

Certainly, start out with ideas on how to sell, and where to target your main efforts, but don't get locked in on those starting points.

Chapter 1: Creating Your Prospect List

Who and where to find prospects will depend on many variables, such as what you're selling, and what the marketplace is like, but here's a checklist to trigger your thinking on sources of leads

1. Obvious or logical users of your product or service.

You probably already know a lot of prospective users of your product or service. You probably already know many of them by name. They may be people you worked with at your previous jobs, or they may be your counterparts in other organizations, or people you know from professional or trade groups.

Others you may not know personally, but know who they are by the organization within which they work, and by their job title. Or you may know that since they hold a particular kind of job, or live in a particular area, or have a particular kind of hobby, they are logical users of your product or service.

Write these names down as they come to you, regardless of how remote the chances of selling them seem now. Develop your list of prospects first, and only later think about narrowing it down. The possibility you list may trigger other ideas, referrals, and leads.

You can set up a simple worksheet to help structure your thinking. List the prospects that occur to you in the left column. Then, in a word or two, sum up in the middle column why you think they are a good prospect. Finally, extend your thinking: given why this seems a good prospect, and why they seem promising, who else is similar?

For example, suppose you have developed an automatic telephone dialer to call and remind patients and clients of upcoming appointments. You developed it with doctors in mind: they are good prospects because they don't want to have gaps in their schedules because patients forgot to come in, nor do they want to create unhappy patients by billing them for those appointments. Your system solves that problem.

But then you expand your opportunities: doctors are not the only prospects. Open up your thinking, spring-boarding from the "Why it's good?" column to other possible prospects. What other businesses or professions don't want to have clients or customers forget appointments? Then you might come up with lawyers, hairdressers, airlines, hotels, even sales people like yourself, who don't want to waste time on calls only to find the prospect has forgotten them.

This is just an example: adapt the worksheet to your own product or service to extend let the "obvious" prospects clue you to those who may be less obvious.

2. Your contacts.

If you're marketing the expertise you gained in your former job, then the people you met while working there -- both within that organization and in other firms -- may be potentials. Similarly, those you met through business and professional groups may be prospects for your services now, or at least may be able to suggest referrals for you to contact.

The people you know in a non-professional way may also be helpful contacts: people from your neighborhood, civic groups, church, circle of friends and acquaintances.

You may ask them for help when you see them face-to-face, or you may decide to phone them for ideas. (You could contact them to get their ideas on potential prospects. Even better, you might ask for their suggestions on your whole business plan. They will be flattered that you asked for their input, and may well have some ideas that had not occurred to you.

3. Referrals.

We'll be discussing the use of referrals later. Ask for referrals from everyone who buys. Even ask for referrals from those who don't buy but nonetheless seem interested in what you offer. (Although they may not have the money or need right now, they may still think you have a worthwhile idea, and want to pass it on to friends.)

To ask for a referral, simply say something to the effect, "By the way, is there anyone else you could suggest I contact?"

If they give you a name, ask, "Do you mind if I mention your name when I call them?" (If you're lucky, they may even offer to call up and make the introduction for you.)

If they have trouble thinking of names, you can gently prompt them by suggesting, "For example, is there anyone else I should talk to in your company (or agency, if it is public sector)?" Pause and wait for an answer. Then prompt, "What about your counterparts in other organizations?"

4. Prospects you attract.

Additional leads may come to you from actions you take including,

- Appearances at trade shows and the like.

- Talks before groups of potential users, such as civic and professional organizations.

- Articles and interviews in trade journals and local media.

- Contacts you make through volunteer work and similar activities.

- Advertisements.

5. "Smokestacking"

The name comes from the old days, when sales people new to a town would begin by driving around looking for the factory smokestacks, as the smokestacks usually indicated where the business in that town was. Nowadays when "smoke-stacking" you would be looking for office buildings, industrial parks, shopping centers, and other clusters of activity that may contain the offices of likely prospects.

Generally, the most efficient way of smoke-stacking these days is to find your way to the Chamber of Commerce, as they will be pleased to supply you with maps, and directories of the businesses, non-profits, and governmental agencies in the area. Most of the time, you'll be able to determine from these lists which organizations are viable prospects, or at least worth further exploration.

Check also if there are regional development agencies in the area, as they would also have directories of manufacturers and other major industries. (The names of these kind of agencies will vary with the state. It may be helpful to call your state's Department of Commerce, or even the Governor's office, as these development or redevelopment agencies or authorities often either use public money, or are funded by state bonds.)

But in some cases it will be helpful to go out and "eyeball" these business clusters, doing some on-site investigation. It may be that the directories are a year or so old, and there may have been turnover. Or some organizations' names may be too vague to tell you what you need to know.

In some cases, you can generate leads by quick "sweeps" through office buildings and commercial clusters, hardly more than poking your head into each office to see if it would be worthwhile to schedule an appointment later. We'll examine the how-to of "sweeping" in Chapter 5.

6. Paper and online research.

This is too vast and variable to get into, but can range from keeping a clipping file of articles from newspapers and magazines to all sorts of gee-whiz stuff to be done on-line.

Summary/Action Plan

Before reading on, spend a few minutes making a first attempt at a concrete action plan to structure your search for prospects. Jot at least three ideas in each category.

1. Who are the "obvious" or "logical" users of your product or service?

2. Your contacts, such as from your previous work, from business and professional groups, from civic, church, and other non-business groups:

3. Initial referrals. At the start, who might be able to help you generate lists of potential users, or make some introductions on your behalf?

4. Attracting prospects. Other than running ads, what inexpensive, feasible ways exist for you to spread the word about yourself and your product?

5. Smoke-stacking. Are there office buildings, industrial parks, and the like where users of your product or service may tend to cluster?

6. Paper and internet research. What publications, directories, membership associations and the like exist in your field that may help you find potential buyers? How can you use the internet to find other prospects?

Chapter 2: Setting Priorities among Prospects

A sure way of failing in anything, especially marketing, is to spread yourself too thin.. The whole world may be prospects for your product or service, but you can't call on everyone first. The taxi-meter is running -- especially in your first months -- so it's crucial to focus on prospects with enough profit potential to make it worth your while.

It's crucial to make conscious choices of which customers are worth calling on personally, and which should best be approached by other, less costly, methods, or written off altogether.

Criteria in setting priorities among potential prospects
In setting priorities, use criteria such as these following, or add you own specific criteria appropriate to your product and your market.

1. The prospect's potential need for your product or service.

In assessing whether a potential should be given high priority, ask yourself exactly how strong this prospect's need is likely to be for your product or service.

Also, is their need for your product likely to be apparent to them at the start, or will you have to develop their awareness of a need? Survival is precarious when your business is just getting started. That's not the time to be fighting lost causes.

Don't hesitate to go for the easy sales first. it is OK to pick the low-hanging fruit. After all, you're in business to make a profit, not to build your character through unnecessary adversity. Some initial successes will ease the financial strain, and give you success stories to use in persuading others.

2. Dollar potential, both short and long term.

As you work, keep the 20/80 principle in mind. From 20 percent of your customers will come 80 percent of your sales and profits. It pays to find that productive 20% as quickly as possible, and focus most of your efforts on them.

But the rule also works in reverse. The other 80 percent of your customers will yield only 20 percent of your sales. That tells you that if you manage your time unwisely, that unproductive 80 percent can eat up your days so you never get around to working with that productive 20 percent.

3. Geographic desirability.

In selling, time is money, and travel is time. In the time that you spend going across town to see one prospect, you could perhaps see four or five other prospects more conveniently located.

On the other hand, the overall objective is to make a profit, not just to save travel time. It may be worth making an "inefficient" trip if that prospect offers the chance for a significant return on the investment of time.

4. "Wedge" potential.

What are the chances that a call on this prospect will result in just a single sale, or will it be likely to open the door for several other sales? For example, it may be worth investing the extra effort to sell to one division of a company if that is reasonably likely to open the way to other divisions.

Similarly, it may be worth investing extra effort to sell to the business leaders in your area, because success with them may open the doors to other prospects.

5. Chances of success, including prospect's reputation for innovation and for working with new suppliers.

Especially in the early days, you're going to be short of capital, and hence operating against a tight deadline before you scrape against the bottom of your money barrel. Downgrade the companies that have a reputation for being slow to change, or for being the last to accept innovation. Experiment with them later, after you have built a reserve cushion.

6. Buying cycle.

Orders by government agencies and other large organizations often are substantial, but may be locked in a year in advance. In addition, there may be mandated buying procedures, such as the requirement to advertise for bids before making any purchases. If these organizations are prime prospects, talk to the contracting officer early, and do the necessary paperwork in time to get on the bidder's lists.

However, take what the contracting officers and others in the agency tell you with a grain of salt. more often than not, there are ways around the rigidities of the purchasing regulations. If you can generate enough interest among the people who will actually be using your product, they, as users, will probably be able to help you through the purchasing red-tape. (We'll be exploring how to do that later in this book.)

Summary

In setting priorities, use criteria such as these; add others appropriate to your market and situation.

1. The prospect's potential need for your product or service.

2. Dollar potential, both short and long term.

3. Geographic desirability.

4. "Wedge" potential.

5. Chances of success/ prospect's reputation for innovation and for working with new suppliers.

6. Buying cycle.

PART TWO: LOCATING AND GETTING THROUGH TO THE APPROPRIATE DECISION MAKER

The central question we address in this Part: Once I find an organization that might be interested, how do I get through to the right person there?

By this point, you have developed a working list of prospects, and have targeted from that list some priority prospects. Now you need to find the name of the specific individual or group within each prospect organization to approach.

That person or team to approach, remember, is what we refer to as the "Prospect" or "Decision Maker" abbreviated DM): that is the individual or team, working in the relevant area, and who has the Authority, Need, and Dollars to enable them to say Yes to what you are offering.

We address the how-to of finding this DM in Chapter 3. Finding the Person or Team Who Can Say Yes.

In Chapter 4. Getting Past the Decision Maker's Screen, we examine some useful methods of either quickly convincing the Screen to put you through to the Decision Maker, or, alternately, of finding a way of getting around the screen to approach the DM directly.

Chapter 5. Cold Calling -- When You Must focuses on the practical how-to for those times when it is appropriate in selling.

Then, in Chapter 6. Convincing the Decision Maker to Meet With You, we address the issue of how to quickly convince the DM to agree to invest time in hearing your message. ("Quickly" is the key: this is not the time for an extended conversation. Busy Decision Makers are reluctant to waste time, either on the phone, or in meetings that threaten to be overly-long.)

Finally, in Chapter 7. Organizing and Learning from Your Phone Calls we point out some ways of improving your telephone techniques.

Chapter 3:   Finding Your Way to the Person or Team Who Can Say Yes

Basic rule: *You can make a sale only if you deal with the person who can say Yes to what you offer.*

Obvious enough. But often overlooked. Organizations are full of people who claim to have decision-making authority.

But in reality most of them have only *negative decision-making authority.* That is, they have the authority to say No to you, But no matter what or how good a deal you offer, they're just not able to say Yes.

People with only negative decision-making authority typically range from the guard at the plant gate, to the Purchasing Manager, to the Decision Maker's secretary or subordinate.

They tend to be easily accessible, so it's tempting to meet with them and get a sense that you're making progress.

But that progress is an illusion. If you do make your presentation to them, you'll generally find that nothing happens -- at least nothing positive. After all, they can't say "Yes, we'll buy." They can only say either "No," or "I'll have to think about it" -- which really means, "I'll carry your message up to my boss, the real decision maker."

Consider the possibilities. First possibility: If they say No, the sale is just as dead as if you had made the case to the right person.

Second possibility: even if they say they'll pass the word on to the real decision maker, it's almost certainly equally dead. Sure, you might be lucky. But the fact is that it's very unlikely that they'll make the kind of strong case for your product or service that you could if you met directly with the Decision Maker.

For one thing, they don't know your product as well as you, and won't be ready to explain why it is better than the competition. Besides, selling your product is not a priority to them: their other responsibilities take first call on time and energy. If the Decision Maker says No, they aren't likely to risk their job by pushing on as you would.

The "Decision Maker"

The "Decision Maker," as we use the term here, is the person (or team) who has the ability to say Yes to what you're offering -- whether that Yes means to buy a product, to hire you or to retain your services, or to take the next step, such as agreeing to a trial run.

In small organizations, the Decision Maker ("DM") will typically be the person at the top -- the owner of a small business, the managing partner of a law firm, the president of a company, the director of a public agency.

It may take more effort to spot the appropriate DM in larger organizations. Begin looking for the appropriate DM early, as soon as you start your preliminary research in developing your prospect list. As you research the company, and particularly as you talk to people both within and outside the organization, keep your antennae open for the person (or work team) who seems to be in charge in the area in which you would propose to work, and who meets the "AND" test.

The "AND" Test

The AND test is this: the Decision Maker is the person (or team) who possesses three key characteristics: Authority, Need, and Dollars (AND).

"A" represents Authority

The person to whom you make your presentation must be at a level to have the authority, or "authorization," to make buying commitments for the amount appropriate to your projected work.

Thus if your cheapest model costs $5,000, and the person with whom you meet has a $3,000 purchasing limit, then you cannot expect a Yes decision from them. That individual, therefore, is not the Decision Maker, in our meaning of the term. He may be a part of a team that has full decision making power. Or he may be a "Decision Influencer" -- that is, somone whose advice is heeded by the actual Decision Maker.

"N" represents Need

Find your way to the person (or department) with a problem that your product or service can solve. That is, find your way to who has the NEED for your product.

If your product is a janitorial cleaning tool, for instance, there is obviously no point in meeting with the head of data processing. Similarly, the purchasing manager is usually the wrong person, as the purchasing manager likely does not have a first-hand need. (We look at the role of the purchasing department later in this chapter.)

"D" represents Dollars

A person can have Authority to buy, and Need for the product, yet still not be a Decision Maker because she lacks Dollars (or budget).

It may not be easy to find whether or not money is available to spend on your product or service. There is no tactful way of straight out asking if they have the money. But you can sometimes ask indirectly, by early questions such as,

"Suppose we find that this product does meet your needs. Will it be possible for you to buy in this present budget cycle?"

However, don't necessarily believe the Decision Maker who claims poverty: usually that's just an excuse to get rid of sales people.

Finding Your Way to the Decision Maker with "AND"

1. Your knowledge of the field.

You may already know from contacts in your professional organization, scuttlebutt in the industry, and your reading of news articles and business journals who's who in the hierarchies of the potential client organization.

But caution: the person who is apparently in charge of an area may not be the person with the necessary AND to make purchases for that area. For instance, the person in charge of the word-processing unit in a firm is probably not the person with the AND to sign off on the purchase of new software or equipment.

In most cases, you may be wiser to avoid talking to that user altogether, and instead go up the chain to the person who has overall responsibility for profitability and productivity in the area relevant to your product or service.

While you could ask this person for guidance on who has Authority, Need and Dollars, there is a risk that, once you open contact with them, you may be locked into making your case to them. From that point, you would be drawn into working with them, rather than directly with the real Decision Maker, with the disadvantages we discussed earlier.

2. Your research within the prospect organization.

This can be the easiest way of all -- if it works. Simply phone the company and ask the operator who is the person in charge of the area that your product relates to. Get the person's name first, then the job title. The title is important, as you need to be sure that this is the manager, and not just a junior clerk.

While you are on the phone, take an extra few seconds to ask who that person reports to -- just in case the decisions are made at the next-higher level.

As you probe for this information, it's usually best not to wave the flag that you are a sales person, as the operator may try to refer you to the purchasing department. You will usually get further if the operator assumes that you are a customer.

If the operator asks why all these questions, you might say simply, "I need to talk to the person in charge of that area." Or, you could admit that you are hoping to sell to the organization, but need to first explore whether there really is a need for your product there. If you are able to establish the right rapport with this receptionist, you may get all the help you need.

Alternately, you might say, "I'm conducting an industry survey" -- which is true, at least in the sense that you are surveying the industry for prospects.

But don't tell any fibs -- because you will be back there later, and they could return to haunt you. Also, do not let the operator connect you to this person yet. At this point you are only determining who they are, and are not yet ready to talk business.

3. Client literature.

A brochure or other company literature, such as an annual report to shareholders, can be a very helpful source of information, as it may give you a better idea of what the organization is "about," what the key themes are there, and perhaps even who's who in the management structure. You might ask the receptionist to send this literature, or you may drop by and pick it up in person.

Actually, dropping by for literature can be a good way of doing some on-site investigation in scouting out the organization as a prospect, as well as in finding who the likely Decision Maker for you product would be.

When you go for the literature, don't go out of your way to say that you are there on a selling mission. A receptionist who assumes that you are a potential customer or shareholder will often be more generous with information. (And if the receptionist recognizes you when you back later on a sales call? Well, plans change, and who can blame you for following up on a business opportunity you chanced upon!)

4. Your network in the organization, or in the industry.

Those whom you meet during your early general "scouting" of the organization may be able to give you a sense of where to make contact.

Your present clients may give you guidance on who their counterparts are with AND buying authority in other firms or agencies. (They may even be willing to make telephone introductions for you, or at least allow you to use them as referrals.)

5. Trade leads with other sales people.

Trade leads with other sales people who work in the same general field, though are not your direct competitors. (That is, if you sell brushes, look to trade leads with those who sell paint.)

6. Business directories and trade groups.

Local directories, perhaps from the Chamber of Commerce may give you the guidance you need. Or, if you're working in a specialized field, determine what trade or professional societies the manager with the responsibility for this area would probably belong to. Phone that society's local or national headquarters to get the directory.

If you will be doing significant selling to those in this field, you might even consider joining the group, provided you are eligible. The time and membership fees you invest will probably pay off in access to a variety of Decision Makers in other organizations. It may also open the way for you to advertise in the group's newsletter. It may even result in your being invited to give a talk or presentation to the group.

7. The internet.

Everything is on the 'net (and more is to come!) You just have to find it.

If You Can't Identify the Decision Maker with AND

Sometimes, no matter what probing and research you do, you still can't determine who actually has Authority, Need, and Dollars within the organization.

Rule of thumb: the person at the very top of the organization will have positive decision making authority, or at least will be able to make things happen by shifting budgets. Even if the top person refers you down, then you have at least opened a channel, so you can later ask to move back upstairs for funding.

Therefore, if in doubt, start as high as possible. If necessary, go to the very top: call the president's office. Chances are, you'll be referred downward. But then you can honestly say, "Mr. Roberts in the President's office suggested I call you."

In a large organization, the person you are directed to may not be the right DM. But, most often, the mistake will be to direct you to the person slightly above the level of the actual DM. But that is typically to your advantage, as you can again benefit from being referred downward, and being able to say you are calling "at the suggestion of" that higher-level person.

It's better to start a level or so too high and be referred downward than to start too low and be locked into a position where you don't have direct contact with the real Decision Maker.

"Decision Influencers"

Even if the user, or the person in charge of an area, does not have the level of Authority, Need, and Dollars to be the actual Decision Maker, they may nonetheless be an important "Decision Influencer."

Decision influencer: even though they can't make the final call, their input and suggestions are listened to with respect. They may have the Need, but Authority and Dollars reside with their boss, or boss' boss. You don't want to offend them by first seeing them, then appearing to skip over their head.

Decision Influencers may include,

The actual users of your product or service. For instance, in mid-sized companies and upward, the person who uses the computer you sell will generally not be the Decision Maker (lacking Authority, Need, or Dollars), but will probably have a significant influence, as they are technically knowledgeable, and will be living with whichever computer is selected.)

Financial advisors such as the firm's accountant or Chief Financial Officer may be Decision Influencers: they may say whether or not the firm can afford what you offer, and may also have input on finance alternatives, such as leasing versus purchasing, and the like.

The Decision Maker's mentor may be a Decision Influencer. That is, the person who has Decision Making Authority, Need, and Dollars, may still want to check it with the "old hand" in the company who has helped him along the way. Chances are, you won't know who that Mentor is, and may never meet them; just be aware there may be one, feeding suggestions, questions and other concerns to the DM.

The Purchasing Manager *may* be a Decision Influencer. That influence may be more on the technical aspects of how to make the purchase happen within the organization's policies on purchasing. But because the Purchasing Manager may have this influence is a good reason not to antagonize him. Go around him to get to the real DM, but do it quietly and in a nice, unobtrusive way.

When TO and NOT TO Begin With the Purchasing Manager

Contrary to what you might expect, it is usually not a good idea to begin your contact with the Purchasing Manager. More often than not, the Purchasing Manager will have clear authority only to say No -- at least with respect to a new product, service, or idea.

In most organizations, the Purchasing Manager's role is to coordinate buying of known commodities. If you're selling copy paper, or paint, or any other kind of standard item the Purchasing Office probably is the place to begin.

But if you're selling something innovative (either because it's a new idea or new product, or because it accomplishes the job in a new way), then you'll be best to find your way to the actual potential user and create the sense of need at that level.

Unconvinced? Project yourself back a couple or three decades, and imagine that you were selling one of the first personal computers. If you had started with the Purchasing Department, they might have said, "Well, we do have a mandate to buy a dozen Selectric typewriters, and a dozen adding machines. But this strange-looking box you're offering clearly isn't a Selectric, and it doesn't fit the specifications we've set up for the adding machine, so we're not interested. Sorry."

But suppose, instead, you had found your way to the head of the engineering department, or to someone in the legal department who had endless versions of the same form to grind out, and had shown just what your little computer could do, then they probably would have found a way to open the necessary doors for you.

That's why I suggest you use the Purchasing Department only as a last resort. (The same goes for the Personnel Department, if you're marketing your services. Instead, find your way to the person or department with the actual need.)

For anything innovative or novel, the Purchasing Manager probably lacks Authority to buy. The Purchasing Manager certainly lacks Need, unless your product happens to be relevant to the Purchasing area. And the Purchasing Manager has Dollars only within prescribed limits.

When it may be good strategy to contact the purchasing manager

There are some occasions when it IS good strategy to contact, or ever begin with, the purchasing manager:

If you cannot otherwise find the person who has AND (Authority, Need, Dollars) to make a positive decision in your field. You can generally best do this by telephone, as you are less likely to be drawn into making a full presentation of what you are offering. This phone contact should be as short as possible, generally not more than about 30 seconds. Here's a model to adapt:

- *"My name is Greta Ross, and I'm with 21st Century Containers. We've developed radically new types of safety containers for shipping fragile or especially valuable items. I know that you firm manufactures computer drives, which are exactly the kind of product suitable for our containers. Who in your organization would you suggest I talk to?"*

If you need to further **clarify** the chain of purchasing command as you "negotiate" your way to the proper Decision Maker: "From our experience, the shipping department is generally not appropriate, as the packaging choice is usually made earlier in the process."

If you know that the wheels are already in motion to buy what you are offering, so the Purchasing Manager has the Authority and

Dollars, and the Need has been communicated from another part of the organization.

To get on the organization's approved list of bidders. (But don't sit around waiting for them to solicit you: continue taking active steps to meet with the appropriate managers, regardless.)

Training Directors: When to and not to begin there

If you are selling "packaged" training products, such as audio or video tapes, or seminars in this year's hot topic, then it is probably productive to start with the organization's Director of Training, or Personnel Director, or Human Relations Coordinator (or similar titles, depending on the organization). They may have Authority, Need, and Dollars for things like that, particularly if your product focuses on areas that have had a lot of publicity, such as employee safety practices.

But what if you are selling not packaged products but rather your consulting services as an expert on this topic (for illustration, employee safety practices). Or suppose you don't think much of the packaged (or "canned") safety training programs that are on the market, and propose to develop custom training specifically for this organization.

In that case, the Training Department might be a dead end. The Training Director probably does not have the Need to improve safety -- at least in any novel way. Thus your best approach would be to bypass the Training and Personnel Departments and find your way to the manager who does have a real reason to be concerned with safety. This may be the company president, who has an incentive to lower insurance costs, or it may be the plant manager.

What if you just can't find the real Decision Maker

Rule of thumb. if you can't spot the real Decision Maker, start at the top of the organization, and let yourself be guided downward. When you contact the suggested person, you can honestly say it is "at the suggestion" of the president (or the office of whoever you contacted).

The time you invest locating the appropriate DM will be worth it. If you call the wrong individual (one too low in the hierarchy, or otherwise lacking Authority, Need, and Dollars) you will often be locked in to dealing with them. You could then move on only at the risk of offending that first contact, who may later turn out to have a significant as an "influencer" of the decision.

While the Purchasing Manager is usually the wrong person (or office) with which to begin your contact, there are some situations in which purchasing is the place to begin.

- When the Purchasing Office seems to be the only source who can tell you who really has Authority, Need, and Dollars.

- When the purchasing apparatus is already in motion, so Need is recognized, the Dollars have been allocated, and now the Purchasing Manager has been delegated Authority to buy.

- When your objective is to get on the organization's list of authorized bidders or suppliers.

Summary

In finding your way to the appropriate Decision Maker for your product, look for the individual or working team with AND:

Authority to make a buying commitment, Need for your product or service, and the Dollars to pay for it.

Your ingenuity is your best tool for finding your way to the right Decision Maker for what you're offering. But here are some starting points:

1. Your knowledge of who's who in the field.

2. Your research in the prospect organization. As you talk to people there, in person or on the phone, stay alert for the clues that can direct you to the person or team with AND.

3. From the client company's literature, such as brochures, annual reports, press clippings, and the like.

4. The network you develop both in this prospect organization, and in the industry.

5. By trading leads with the other sales people you meet -- those who cover the same ground as you, though with non-competing products.

6. Business directories, trade groups, the internet.

Chapter 4:   Getting Past the Decision Maker's Screen

People with the kind of positive decision making authority you need if you are to make the sale--- that is, who have Authority, Need, and Dollars --- tend to be busy people with many responsibilities. To minimize interruptions, they often set up various types of "Screens" around themselves. (We'll honor these Screens with capital letters here!)

Screens may extend from the security guard at the gate, to the telephone receptionist, to the executive secretary who guards the door to the DM's office. The Screen's function is to minimize distractions so the Decision Maker can focus on what is truly significant to the well-being of the organization.

That means that the Screen will open for you if, and only if, you communicate, through your words and professionalism, that you have the potential of bringing something of significant value to the organization. That is, if you present a sound business purpose for seeing the Decision Maker.

How can you get that sense of significance across before the Screen's mind clicks shut? We'll examine some techniques in this chapter. But first we need to address the important question of . . .

Whether to "Cold Call" or Work by Appointment

It's easy enough to "cold-call" (that is, drop in at Decision Makers' offices in the hope of slipping in at convenient intervals). But sales people who rely on cold-calling waste a lot of productive time waiting in reception rooms, and driving to meetings that never take place because the DM couldn't fit them in.

You have only so many good hours in a business day: is the best use of those hours waiting for other people's meetings to end so you can have a few minutes to make your presentation?

Investing the time to phone ahead for your appointments pays off in several ways:

- It projects to the DM a business-like respect for the value of time, both your own and that of the Dm.

- By making a fixed appointment, you set up an environment that permits some control over the proceeding, free from phone calls and interruptions.

- It allows you to better prepare for the meeting, since you know for sure who you will be meeting, you can take the time to do a little more research in advance.

- In some situations, you have no real choice other than to work by appointments, since executives with real decision making power often can seen only by appointment.

Getting through (or around) the screen

Whether you choose to cold-call or to phone ahead for appointments, you still need to get past the Screen so you can talk directly to the Decision Maker. Here are some methods to get you started, useful both in phoning and cold-calling in person.

1. Whenever possible, make your contact through referrals or other kinds of "pre-introductions."

If you are calling this DM at the suggestion of another of your clients or of a mutual friend, make that clear at the very start, both to the Screen, and later to the DM: *"I'm calling at the suggestion of Peter Wenders of GMR Industries."*

If you already know the Decision Maker from another context, mention this to the Screen, but be careful how you word it. You don't want the Decision Maker to come to the phone -- or to avoid you -- because he thinks you're setting up a tournament at the country club, or asking for a donation to the college alumni fund.

Flag that other context as a door-opener in the Screen's mind, but then quickly move on to your present business purpose. Here's a good model to follow:

- *"At the Rotary luncheon the other day, I was talking with Ms. Tompkins. I later came upon an idea that I realized might be helpful to her work here. I'd like to set a time to drop by and explain it to her. I wonder if you can help me arrange a time, please?"*

- Or, *"Mr. Parsons dropped by our booth at the NATL show, and asked me to get in touch with him to arrange a meeting to explore some possibilities he saw there. I have the information ready now. Do you think Wednesday morning or Thursday afternoon would be more convenient for him?"*

2. Make the Screen your ally.

When you phone an organization, listen closely to the name of the person who answers. It may be someone you met earlier when you were on the premises researching the organization as a potential client. If the name is familiar, remind them of your previous conversation:

> ▪ *"Mrs. Johnson, this is Jack Thomas of Computers for Business. You may remember me from my visit to your office last week." (Pause a moment to give thinking time.) "We spoke at that time about how your organization handles inventory. Since then, I've had a chance to give some more thought to what we discussed. I have some ideas that I think Mr. Rabin will find of interest. Perhaps you could schedule an appointment for me with him. It should take about 20 minutes at most. I'm available both Tuesday morning and Wednesday afternoon. Would either of these times be convenient for him to meet?"*

If the questions you asked during that earlier conversation were well-focused, perhaps suggesting problem areas for which you might offer a solution, then you may have intrigued the Screen, raising the thought that perhaps you have the potential of solving a problem with which they are familiar.

For example, if one of your questions was, "Do you have crunch periods during the month when you're very overloaded?" the DM's secretary may assume that you have a remedy available, and hence will be eager to put you through to the boss.

3. "Pre-sell" the Screen. But speak only in broad concepts. Do not become drawn into the details.

In persuading the Screen to put you through to the DM, you'll obviously need to talk some about your business purpose for calling. But beware of saying too much.

Granted, this puts you on the horns of a dilemma. If you are too vague, you will not get the appointment. But, conversely, the more you talk of the specifics of what you are offering, the more reasons you'll give the Screen for keeping you out: "You work with computers, you say? Well, there's no point in your seeing Mr. Chase, as we already have our own in-house computer expert."

Keep in mind the basic principle: You can't *make* the sale over the phone, but you *can lose* it on the phone.

Therefore, when you're on the phone, speak in overall conceptual terms of what your product or service WILL DO FOR the organization, not of what it IS, nor of its technical features.

Thus if your consulting focus is on introducing computer systems for increasing productivity, do not say "computers." Instead, speak of "methods for increasing productivity," or "techniques for developing more efficient work-flows."

In explaining to the Screen, focus your communication beyond what your product or service IS in order to speak of what it CAN DO FOR the purchaser. For example, if your specialty is training in telephone marketing, you could say,

- *"We've been able to help organizations extend their marketing reach to smaller customer accounts, and those in hard-to-reach places. As a result, we typically help our clients increase sales by 15 to 20%."*

Notice in this example that there is no mention at all of "telephone," and no mention of "training." But since you're offering the prospect of increasing sales by 20%, how could a Screen reasonably turn you away?

Here are some models you can adapt:

- *"I'd like to speak to Mr. Dobson about some methods that may be able to increase your organization's productivity by ten-percent or more, as we have with other firms."*

- Or, *"I'm a design consultant, and I'd like to propose some suggested designs for Ms. White to consider for your next series of advertisements."*

- Or, *"I represent a consulting firm that specializes in financial management. We've worked with a number of organizations like yours, and I believe that we may be able to help you. I do need to speak with Ms. Jensen to find out what your present needs are, and in what directions you'll be moving in the next couple of years."*

4. Ask questions the Screen won't be able to answer.

The way to get through the Screen is to communicate that you have a sound business reason for talking to the DM -- one that will help the DM or the organization work better.

Thus if the Screen is putting you on the defensive with questions, switch from defense to attack by asking your own questions, as in this dialogue:

Screen: "And what is it you want to talk to Mr. Builder about?"

Sales person: "Mr. Builder **is** the construction engineer on the PDM Center, isn't he?"

Screen: "Yes, of course. But why do you need to talk to him?"

Sales person: "I'm calling to determine whether the PDM Center is being built in accord with the NEPA Standards on hydro-thallaxic transfaxions."

Screen: "I have no idea. For that you'll have to talk to Mr. Builder. Hold, please."

With a little ingenuity you can come up with a repertoire of unanswerable questions like these. The questions should be relevant to the reason for your call to the DM, but a little more technical or detailed than a receptionist or secretary would be willing to address.

5. If necessary, call when the Screen is away.

If you find that you just can't break through the Screen, try phoning before or after normal business hours, or even over the lunch hour: Key Decision Makers are typically at their desks earlier, or later, or both, to take advantage of the quiet time when the office is empty.

In off hours, Decision Makers often answer their own phones. If you do get the DM on the line, be particularly brief and to-the-point, respecting that she is in the office at this time precisely in order to avoid interruptions.

Watching for the Screen's "buying signals"

Be attuned for the subtle clues that indicate that the Screen is relaxing the barrier. When you sense this opening, don't hesitate. Use the momentum that you've built up, and move on to ask for what you want, which is, ultimately, to meet with the DM.

In some organizations, the Screen is authorized to set up the appointment, and can write you onto the calendar without your needing to speak to the DM at this point.

That's ideal, as it means you don't have to make your case again to the DM over the phone. If you sense this may be the case, work on the assumption, and suggest to the Screen a pair of alternative times from which to choose:

"I'm free to meet Mr. Bolger next Tuesday afternoon. Or would Thursday morning be better?"

Just what these buying signals consist of will depend a lot on the individual's own mannerisms. Here are some to watch for; in time you will develop a sixth-sense for when the mood has changed.

- **Change in phone manner**. The Screen may be less formal, less curt, or may become more informal and relaxed.

- **Questions may be buying signals**. Watch for the switch from questions about the product (which are basically looking for reasons to say No), to questions that relate to practical things like where you are located, or when you can come in.

- **Some statements may be indirect buying signals**. A Screen who says, "Mr. Watkins is out of town all this week," is, consciously or not, telling you that you've won, and it's now just a matter of settling on a mutually-convenient time. If so, stop making your case, and say something to the effect, "Fine. I'll be in your area next Tuesday and Thursday. Which would be better?"

- Sometimes **the level of interest** in what you are selling is a buying signal. Listen for subtle clues. If you're selling, for example, productivity improvement software for the office, the Screen might probe for reasons to say No. But the Screen might also be wanting to know more because he is very eager for a way of easing his own workload. Often, the difference will be perceptible in voice tone, energy, and enthusiasm -- perhaps even in the kinds of questions. If the questions are somewhat technical, that may be a clue that they have already begun looking for something like you offer.

When you encounter voice-mail

It's increasingly likely that you will encounter voice-mail or answering machines when you call the Decision Makers in both small organizations and large. Think through in advance just how you will respond.

Will you leave a message, or keep trying to reach the DM directly? If you leave your name, then it is in the DM's hands to respond, and you lose control. If the DM doesn't return your call, then it gets awkward: does that mean no interest, or just too busy? But sometimes leaving your name and number is the only way. Besides, if the DM does call you back, that puts you in a good position, as it shows some level of interest.

As a rule, I try several times, not leaving my name, hoping to finally get the DM at the desk. If the pattern becomes clear that I'm not likely to catch the person, then I do go ahead leave my name and number, figuring that this way there is at least a chance of getting to the DM.

But don't "wing" your messages. Decide just what message you want to leave, then boil it down so it gets quickly to the point. Rehearse your message until you can say it confidently and with a smile in your voice.

Then, before leaving your first message on a prospect's voice-mail, call your own and leave the same message. Then go back and revise and rehearse it again until it is right.

Whether to identify your company, or reason for calling, is something for you to work out, with experience. If the DM thinks you are a potential buyer of his services, she will be more likely to return the call than if she knows you are selling to her. On the other hand, a busy DM may not bother returning calls that lack information. Definitely do not try to make the sale, or even describe your product, over voice mail. Just say who you are, maybe your company, and your phone number. If you are out a lot, you could suggest ideal times to call.

Summary

Cold-calling -- that is, arriving cold at the prospect's office -- is usually not a productive way of using your time.

In most situations, it will be worth the investment of effort to set up at least a few definite sales appointments each day. (If you have spare time around scheduled appointments, you can use that for cold-calling.)

When you phone for an appointment, you may find that the person who actually has Authority, Need and Dollars is surrounded by a "secretarial Screen" who makes it hard to get through and ask for an appointment.

To get through the Screen, convince them that you are bringing the organization something of significant value. Methods for accomplishing this include:

1. Use referrals from satisfied clients who have recommended you to this organization and this decision maker.

2. Make the Screen your ally by outlining in conceptual terms how you may be able to help the organization.

3. "Pre-sell" the screen. But speak only in broad concepts. Do not become drawn into the details. You can only lose the sale over the phone, but cannot make the sale.

If possible, get the Screen to put you on the Decision Maker's calendar without your having to talk to him at this time.

If the Screen continues to block you, try more creative methods of getting through to the DM.

4. If necessary, ask questions you expect the Screen won't be able to answer.

5. Call when the Screen is away, perhaps before or after the normal working hours, in hopes of catching the Decision Maker directly.

Concluding note: on playing the percentages

When you call the Screen, and at every other point in the selling process, you risk hearing "No." Nobody likes to hear No, not even long-time professional sales people.

But you need to look at the noes you hear in perspective:

Selling is a percentage game. It would be unrealistic to expect that every attempt would result in a sale. But there are sales out there waiting to be discovered. Success in selling is, to a large extent, getting through the No's to find the Yes responses.

"No" is useful feedback, from which you can build a sale. The key is to probe that No, so you know precisely what it means here and now, in this specific situation, coming from this unique individual.

Very often, once you know that, you can overcome it using methods we'll examine later in this book.

Chapter 5: Cold-Calling — When You Must

For the reasons discussed in the previous chapter, cold-calling -- dropping in on prospects without an appointment -- is usually not a good use of your time. You can waste a lot of productive time waiting for an opening to see the Decision Maker.

Besides, that kind of willingness to wait for an opening might be interpreted by the DM as an indication that you don't have anything better to do with your time.

But there *are* certain situations in which cold-calling IS appropriate.

Cold-calling **is** *appropriate for follow-up calls on existing customers,* when you drop by to make sure all is going well with your product. (We'll examine follow-up customer-care calls more in Chapter 30).

Cold-calling **may** *be a productive use of time if* you find yourself with time to spare between other appointments. Since you're in an area, it's a good use of that open time to prospect for new leads. Cold-calling is ideal for seeing what other opportunities are in that part of your territory.

In some cases, you may just get lucky and stumble upon a qualified Decision Maker who is interested in meeting right then. If so, seize the opportunity. (If the DM is interested but doesn't have the time then, at least move at that point to set up an appointment for another day or time.)

Cold-calling can be useful as a tool for conducting some kinds of preliminary research and scouting for prospects. To quickly survey potential for your product or service among the tenants of an office building or industrial park, the best way may be to quickly "sweep" from office to office, gathering information.

This third use of cold-calling as a research method is the focus of this chapter.

Earlier, we looked briefly at "smoke-stacking" and "sweeping" buildings in order to rapidly scan and flush out potential prospects. In those sweeps, you speak briefly with the receptionist or secretary to make a quick determination of whether it is worth calling back to see the Decision Maker.

Just what information you are looking for at this early stage will vary with your product and the market. The checklist below is a starting point; adapt it to your own uses.

Note: As you meet with people during these initial "sweeps" for information, the tone should be that of a *conversation*, not an *interrogation*. Be friendly. Don't put them on the spot with a barrage of questions.

If someone is reluctant to talk, it could be that they are only a temporary employee and doesn't want to admit it. Or it may be that they don't want to give away too much information without knowing why you're there, and what you're going to do with this information

To overcome this, put yourself clearly in context without getting into much detail (you don't want to be drawn into making your sales call to this person who can only say No, but not Yes. Here are some ways of setting context:

- You could say that you have an innovative product that you think may be able to help this firm, but need to get some preliminary information to determine whether to ask the Decision Maker for some time.

- Or, you could mention that you are planning a "VIP Seminar" or exhibition. You want to send an invitation to the DM in this organization, but need to make sure that their attendance would be appropriate.

The kinds of information to be looking for when cold calling

What the organization does. Not every company or agency name is clear. "Automatex" may not give a clue to whether or not the firm can use your product. Governmental agencies can be even more obscure: ever pass the local "Human Services Center" and get an image of humans up on racks getting their oils changed? (Would that be corn oil or codfish oil?)

- *How large the organization is* may be relevant in some situations.

- *Whether this is the headquarters or a branch operation of another organization.* Depending on your product and its cost, buying decisions might only be made at the headquarters office.

- *If possible, the name of the key Decision Maker.* The guard or receptionist may or may not know.

- The exact address and phone number of this office, so you can easily check back later.

Checklist of how-to's when doing cold-call "sweeps"

As you arrive at the building or office park, begin by checking the tenant directory. If you already have a list, such as from the Chamber of Commerce, check it against the tenant directory to make sure the addresses are still current.

Also, jot down the office number of any others with names that hint they may be particularly worth calling on -- so that you don't inadvertently pass by those offices as you move through.

Work systematically as you sweep the area. If it's a building, start at the top and work downwards. (That way, you can easily walk down between floors, and save the time of waiting for the elevator.)

Some buildings will have security guards. If you're in business dress, you shouldn't have a problem if you walk briskly, projecting that you're there on an appointment.

Some buildings have special security, and will let you in only if you have a confirmed appointment. To get around that, some sales people set up one appointment, then sweep the rest of the building on the way out. The security people may not be pleased, but it may be your only way in.

1. Make sure you're wearing a friendly smile as you enter each door. (Granted, this can be hard at the start, when you're on-edge wondering what lurks behind these strange doors.) First impressions count, and a smile can put even the most hard-bitten security guards and receptionists at ease.

Project yourself into the guard or receptionist's shoes, sitting there all day, with not much happening. They may not even have a window. You -- a sales person coming through that door -- may be the most exciting thing that has happened in the past hour, so bring some sunshine with you.

2. Keep your eyes open. Even before you enter the building, a glace at the place, and the vehicles outside, can tell you a lot. Once inside a particular office, the kind of equipment and furnishings can give helpful clues. Does the place look prosperous? Is there a hum of energy in the air? Are there product samples in the reception area, or advertising posters framed on the wall that give you a quick reading of what the place is about?

3. Make a mental note of the receptionist's name. It will smooth the present conversation, and will be helpful if you phone back later for an appointment. Then you can say, "Mrs. Wilkins, this is Rhonda Prost. We talked the other day ..."

As soon as you leave each office, take a few moments to transfer your mental notes of names, impression and facts onto paper. Otherwise, by the end of the day all will be a blur.

4. Begin in a low-key way by saying something on the order of, "I wonder if you can help me?" There's something about asking for help: you immediately you become less threatening. After all, most people like to help.

When they say "Sure, I'll try," respond on the order of, "I was in the building for another meeting, and was intrigued by your company name. What does Automatex do?"

At this point, the guard or receptionist doesn't know who you are, or why you're there. You could be a potential client of their firm, so they will generally tell you enough for you to determine whether it is worth pursuing further.

If you sense that you have arrived at a bad time -- because things seem to be in crisis with a deadline or the like -- apologize, and offer to come back another time. Before leaving, ask when would be a good time to stop in again.

5. If the organization looks promising, ask for the name of the person who is likely to be the Decision Maker for your product: "I don't want to see him or her now, but can you tell me who's in charge of _____."

6. Chances are the receptionist will tell you without any hesitation. But at about this point, may begin asking you some questions about who you are, and why you're there. Your best response is, "I'm in the _____ industry, and I may want to contact Ms. Decision Maker with some ideas."

Notice that when you say you're in the _____ industry, you don't flag yourself as a sales person. You're just "in the industry." The receptionist may still be thinking that you are a potential customer. and since you're not asking for any of the Decision Maker's time now, you'll probably get the name and information you ask for.

7. If you don't have any idea of who the Decision Maker might be for your product area--such as from the kind of job title that would probably be appropriate—you can probe the receptionist. "Can you tell me, who here is responsible for (fill in)?"

It can be difficult to put into words just what person or job title you're looking for. It may help to speak of the general area of the need your product can fill.

8. After the receptionist suggests a name, echo that name, and ask what the person's title is. This is a way to double-check, in case the receptionist has directed you to the user of the product, rather than the actual Decision Maker.

When you have that name and title, take it up one more step "And who does Mr. Simpson report to?" Then ask for that person's title.

The receptionist may not know the formal titles ("I don't know his actual title, but he's in charge of _____"). Whatever you get is at least a start, and will be useful later when you phone back either to ask for an appointment, or to probe further to find just where Authority, Need, and Dollars reside.

9. Note that in this approach, you have not mentioned your name or firm. That is intentional. It's generally best not to volunteer your firm name yet, at that might flag that you are there hoping to sell, not buy from them.

10. If the organization still looks promising, try to collect literature to review later for further leads and clues. If you see a business-card dispenser on the counter, take one. Ask the receptionist if you might have a brochure or other company literature, such as an annual report to shareholders. Materials like these can be helpful sources of information, giving you an idea of what the organization is "about," what the key themes are there, and perhaps even who's who in the management structure.

11. If the chemistry of this initial call went particularly well, it may be productive for you to leave your business card. That will serve as a pre-introduction later. On the other hand, if you had a difficult time with the receptionist, then try to avoid leaving the card, or even your name. That way, you can let a couple of weeks pass before phoning back, and may not even be remembered. Or a different person may be on the front desk.

12. Be prepared for good luck. Even though you are not looking to make your presentation now, things can happen. The DM may be within earshot as you talk with the receptionist and come out to find out what's happening. Or the receptionist may not feel comfortable answering questions, and may ring someone up the organizational ladder to come out.

Even though you are planning only to do a quick sweep, carry your usual sales essentials of note-pad, order blanks, and whatever literature or samples you need.

13. Nobody likes rejection, but it can happen that some guards or receptionists will refuse to tell you much. Don't take it personally: they were probably just as nasty to the last person who called. Move on. There are other prospects. And other ways of getting the information from this organization, despite that receptionist.

Sample script for cold-call sweeps

Here's an outline of a sample script you can adapt, to get you started. (It's useful as a model for cold calling both in person and over the phone.)

(SR is Sales Rep; REC is receptionist, guard, etc.)

SR: "Hello. I wonder, perhaps you could help me?"

REC: "I'll try. What do you need?"

SR: "I noticed your firm's name on the building directory, and I was intrigued by what field you're working in."

REC: (Explains briefly, and SR recognizes that this may be promising.)

SR: "Is this the main headquarters of the company, or a branch location?"

REC: "This is all there is."

SR: "Is all of the firm's data processing (or whatever your field is) done here?"

REC: "That's correct."

SR: "That's the business I'm in -- data processing. Can you tell me who's responsible for it here?"

REC: "That would be Mr. Simmons."

SR: "Mr. Simmons. And what's his title?"

REC: "Supervisor of data processing."

SR: (Recognizes that the supervisor of DP is probably not going to be the Decision Maker with Authority, Need, and Dollars. The appropriate DM will be further up the organizational chart.) *"Who does Mr. Simmons report to?"*

REC: "His boss would be Ms. Jane Whitely."

SR: "And her title?"

REC: "Vice-president of operations. She reports to Dr. Grafton, our president."

SR: "I'd like to give Ms. Whitely a call sometime, because I think we may have some areas of mutual interest. What would her phone extension be? Do you happen to have her business card handy?"

REC: *"Of course."*

SR: "Thank you for the help. I'd like to leave you my card, as I'll probably be calling in the next few days. And, by the way, do you have a company brochure I could have? Or any other literature that might help me get a sense of the organization?"

If building security prevents "sweeps"

Some buildings discourage sweeping or "canvassing." Here's how one marketer gets the job done, regardless:

1. Find out the major firms or best products for your product in advance. Even if the security guard won't let you wander through the building, there should be no problem with letting you see the directory.

2. Phone these best prospects and ask for the phone number of their fax machine.

3. Drive to the building, fire up your laptop computer and your cellular phone, and zap an introductory letter to the appropriate manager in each of these firms. (It will be a standard letter, prepared in advance, onto which you plug address information.) In the letter, say you will be phoning them within the next two hours.

4. When the first batch of letters are off, begin phoning the people to whom you sent the letters. Say something to the effect, "I faxed you a letter a few minutes ago explaining who I am. I'm in the area now, and would like to come by to introduce myself briefly, and to learn about you and your organization. I'd expect the meeting should take about ten minutes at the most. Would right now be good, or would it be better to meet in, say, an hour or two?"

5. Don't be surprised if some of the prospects want to come and meet you at your car to check out your system!

If a car fax and cellular phone are not practical for you, you can fax the letters overnight, then call from a pay phone in the lobby. (This tip adapted from an article in *Success* on a technique used by Orlando sales training consultant Gordie Allen.)

Chapter 6: Convincing the Decision Maker to Meet With You

Once you get past the Screen and have the Decision Maker on the phone, you have one crucial objective to accomplish: to persuade that DM to invest time in meeting face-to-face with you.

Caution: Time is money to effective Decision Makers, and they are not inclined to waste it either in long phone calls or in unproductive meetings.

When you speak with the DM, be friendly but get to the point. This is not the time to chat about the weather or how the day is going. Nor is it the time to talk in detail of what your product is, nor of your background.

"Call up. Fix up. Hang up."

Sales professionals think of this first phone contact as the "Call up, fix up, hang up" phase. The point is to make the call, arrange a meeting, then get off the line without getting bogged down.

You don't want to seem brusque during the conversation, but you also don't want to get into a long conversation at this point. For busy Decision Makers, phone calls are, by nature, interruptions, so the shorter and the more to-the-point the interruption is, the better.

There's another important reason for being succinct now:

- you can lose the chance to meet with the DM if you talk too much, but ...

- no matter what you say, *you cannot make the sale* over the phone.

Once the DM picks up the phone, you have two crucial tasks to accomplish in perhaps 30 seconds or less . . . that is, before the DM's interest flags, or before another in-coming call takes priority. In these opening seconds, you need to,

First, introduce yourself and your company, (if you operate under a company name), and,

Second, present concise reasons for your phone call, as well as for why the Decision Maker should invest time in meeting with you.

That may seem a lot to accomplish in 30 seconds, but it can be done, as in this model script. Adapt it to your situation.

- *"Mr. Robinson, this is Tom Gibbons of Productivity Services. I'm calling because I believe we can increase your firm's profitability by reducing office overhead -- perhaps by as much as 20% in the first year. I'd like to meet with you for about a half hour to explore the possibilities. Would later this week be convenient, or would early next week be better for you?"*

Useful "Hot-Buttons" in this First Phone Contact

Before you dial the call, try to have at least one of these classic hot-buttons ready to lead with, and another in reserve:

1. You are following up on a personal referral from someone the DM knows and respects.

This also tends to be a very powerful door-opener. But be sure to pronounce the referral's name and organization clearly, so the DM makes the connection quickly. Here's a model to adapt:

- *"My firm has recently completed a project with Lucas Industries, and Mr. Lucas suggested that we contact you. He felt that we may have areas of mutual interest. Perhaps he has already talked to you about this?"*

2. Highlight key relevant cases from your successful track record.

Again, be succinct. Talk "bottom-line." That is, emphasize what these cases imply you can DO FOR the DM's organization, not the technical details of the product or service you offer.

These first models are appropriate if you already have experience that is directly on-target.

- *"We've been able to help a number of other law firms in the area reduce their overhead costs. This translates into an average of ten-percent greater profitability. I'd like to meet with you to explain how we may be able to help your firm, as well."*

- Or, *"As an art consultant, I work with several other people in the Great Falls area who are interested in art for both aesthetic and investment reasons. In about 15 minutes together we can determine whether this is appropriate for you."*

- Or, *"I design training programs, and have recently worked with two large banks in the mid-west. As a consultant to these banks, I developed teller training that increased the productivity of tellers by over fifteen percent. I believe I can do the same for your bank. I'd like to meet with you for a half-hour to explore the possibilities."*

But suppose you don't yet have independent experience to refer to? That is, what if all your work has been as an employee, and not as a consultant or self-employed? One approach is to modify your lead-in. Thus you could rephrase the last model above as,

- *"When I was at BigBank, I headed a team that developed teller training that increased productivity by . . ."*

Alternately, if you have just set up your business and don't yet have successes to refer to, you can suggest a potential need area, leaving it to the DM to infer that you have the necessary capability for meeting it successfully:

- *"As you know, one of the most troublesome problems facing most law firms is how to store and access key data. We can offer you a solution that will both save your firm a significant amount of money the first year, and increase your access to this information."*

- *Or, "I'm an art consultant. I believe it would be worth your time to meet with me for a half-hour at your convenience to discuss a program I offer, as I think it may have significant investment potential for you."*

3. BRIEFLY outline what you believe you can do for this organization.

Again, to capture the DM's interest, emphasize what you can DO FOR the DM's organization, not the details of what you (or your product) DO.

This must be a concise, "netted-out" statement, usually not more than a couple or three sentences. You will lose the DM's attention if you are too long-winded. Here's a model to adapt:

- *"I'm calling because I have ideas to share on how my firm may be able to reduce your turnaround time on receivables."*

Notice how this model script is designed to intrigue the potential client through a mention of an area of interest -- how you can speed up payments, and hence improve cash flow and profitability. It DOES NOT get into the technical wizardry of the software program you have developed and hope to install.

Your earlier homework in researching the organization may trigger some initial ideas on ways in which you may be able to help:

- *"My readings on the difficulties your firm is having in keeping up with demand for your products indicated to me that . . ."*

Or, raise suggestions from your experience of how organizations like this may need help:

- *"I've been able to help a number of emerging firms like yours, and it's been my experience that you may be experiencing certain typical difficulties in this stage of your growth."*

Do not get bogged down at this point in the details of how you will do what you propose to do: leave that for the face-to-face meeting.

4. Explain that you are calling to provide information the DM requested earlier.

If you are calling in response to the DM's request for information, that clearly is a door-opener. But as you lead with it, be sure to make the point clearly that you are following up on a request, as well as the context in which that request was made:

"We met following my talk last week before the local BOE Association, and you asked me if I had ever heard of the method being applied to your industry. The question intrigued me, and I researched it, and came up with some interesting results. I'd like to meet with you to share these findings. Would an afternoon later this week, or early next week be convenient?"

If the DM presses for more detail at this stage

But what if the DM asks for more detail on just what it is you do, or how your approach differs from that of your competition?

In the first place, you want to avoid getting drawn into too much detail, since you can't make the sale over the phone, but can lose it. Yet you can't very well refuse to answer the question, as the DM would likely then refuse to see you.

The key is to speak in terms of overall concepts -- especially end-results -- without getting into the technical details. Here's one model for handling it without offending the DM:

- *"Ultimately I'm a problem solver. What I suggested a moment ago is only one of a variety of ways in which I may be able to help your organization. Based on my research, I'm willing to come to your office and invest a half-hour of my time to explore these areas of need together. Are mornings or afternoons better for you?"*

However, the DM may be asking for additional details with the idea of distinguishing you from your competitors. Generally you will sense if this is the case by the nature of the questions asked. The more sophisticated the questions, the greater the likelihood that one of your competitors has already "educated" this DM. If that's the case, then respond succinctly, highlighting the advantages of your approach.

As much as possible, focus on the positive "bottom-line" benefits of your approach -- greater ease of use, or improved productivity, efficiency, profitability — rather than the technical nuances. What matters to the DM, remember, is not so much what your product IS as what it DOES for him and his situation.

Setting a time for the meeting

Sometimes, of course, you'll have to take whatever time-slot the DM offers. But with a little pre-planning, you can usually nudge the time into a slot that is convenient for both the DM and yourself.

By planning ahead and having convenient times ready to suggest, you can group several meetings in the same geographic area, and hence avoid the wheel-spin of running in circles to meetings all over town.

In suggesting a meeting time, experienced sales people generally offer the DM an alternate choice, asking her to select between options. This usually proves to be an efficient way of settling on a mutually convenient time.

Some models for phrasing the choices:

- "Would you prefer to meet late this week or early next?"

- Or, "Are mornings or afternoons generally better for you?"

- Or, "Would Tuesday morning or Wednesday afternoon be more convenient?"

Try to offer a range of choices, such as the morning one day, and the afternoon another day; or late one week versus early the next.

If there seems to be no mutually convenient time, suggest the noon hour. Many Decision Makers choose to eat at the desk, to gain a quiet time relatively free from incoming phone calls and other interruptions.

If the Decision Maker seems interested but is still unable to fit you into her schedule, ask, "What time do you come in in the morning?" and offer to meet then. (Although you could also suggest meeting after the normal hours, it's usually not as good a time, as both of you may be tired at the end of the day.)

"Should anyone else be present?"

Despite your earlier efforts to ensure that you have contacted the appropriate DM -- that is, the person or team with the appropriate Authority, Need, and Dollars -- it's nonetheless possible that you have come in at the wrong level.

A subtle way of testing whether this really is the ultimate decision maker is to ask, after you've settled on a time to meet, "Is there anyone else who should be present?"

The question is a subtle reminder for them to think whether someone from the next level up should be present to bring either Authority or Dollars. Or whether the actual user, perhaps their subordinate, should also be invited to attend.

It's not likely to happen, but if this apparent Decision Maker takes offense to your question, as seeming to doubt his authority, you can explain that you want to be sure to bring enough materials, or that you like to get a sense of how large a group you'll be talking with.

Closing the Call

Once you have the appointment, get off the phone as quickly as you can without seeming brusque. The longer you linger, the greater the risk that the Decision Maker may change his mind about seeing you.

But there are three matters that should be attended to before you hang up.

First, make sure that the Decision Maker actually records this appointment in his book. You don't want to arrive and find that he forgot the appointment, and left for the day. One subtle way of accomplishing that: repeat the date and time of the appointment, to confirm that you're both in agreement, then say, "I'm jotting it in my appointment book now. Tuesday March second at ten." By mentioning that, you subtly cue the DM to do the same.

Second, make sure that the Decision Maker has your phone number, so he can contact you in case something comes up. While it does open up a risk that the DM could call to cancel, it reduces the risk of your wasting time on a useless trip across town.

Third, if you need detailed directions to the office, suggest that the DM transfer you to the secretary or receptionist: he will appreciate your not taking up his time.

If you are not sure about this firm or this Decision Maker

In this Chapter, we've been working on the assumption that you are sure that this firm is a good prospect, and that this is the right Decision Maker.

But what if you're not sure? If the call is convenient enough to make -- in terms of location, travel, etc. -- it may be best to take your chances and see how it works out.

But calls are expensive in the time and travel invested. If you can't make this call easily while in the area for another, then it's worth asking some screening questions before you push for the appointment. What those questions are will depend on your particular product and industry.

The model script will give you some ideas on how to approach it. (SR is Sales Rep, and DM this potential Decision Maker.)

SR: "Mr. Hopkins? This is Tina Rogers of TGR Associates. I'm calling because I believe we can increase your firm's pproductivity by reducing office overhead -- perhaps by as much as 20% in the first year. But at this point, I'm frankly not sure if there is an appropriate mesh between our services and your needs. I'd like to ask you a few very brief questions. It'll take about two minutes. Is this a good time, or would it be better if I called back later?"

DM: "Now is fine, provided it's just a couple of minutes."

SR: "I have done some initial research. Let me begin by confirming some of the things I've learned, just to be sure they are accurate. I understand that you're the managing partner at your firm, and that part of your area of responsibility is to oversee all expenditures relating to the operation of the office. Is that basically right?"

DM: "Basically. There are some aspects I would clear with the management board."

SR: "If the firm were to upgrade computer systems, would that be your area of responsibility?"

DM: "That would depend. If it's software relating to office operations that's my area -- things such as accounting systems, word processing, and the like. But if it comes to the software on the professional side, such as specialized design software, then that would be handled by the partner in charge of professional operations."

SR: "I see. Well, I 'm thinking that may be the person I need to talk to. That's the partner in charge of professional operations -- is that the actual title? And what was their name?"

Notice that in probing for information, you do open yourself up for more questions back from the person you're talking to.

There is the risk that they may hear enough to decide that they don't want to meet with you, even though you find that you do want to meet with them, after all.

But that's the chance you take, and perhaps it is better to risk losing some over the phone than to waste time on sales calls that may not be appropriate.

Summary

When you get through the Decision Maker's Secretarial Screen, you come into the "Call up. Fix up. Hang up" phase. It IS the time to briefly introduce yourself and ask for an appointment to meet. It is NOT the time to get into prolonged explanations, or to try to make the sale over the phone.

To quickly spark the DM's interest to the point of granting an appointment, you can,

1.   Explain that you are following up on a personal referral from someone the DM knows.

2.   Briefly highlight your successes with other clients.

3.   Briefly sketch what you believe you may be able to do for the DM's organization, based on your related experience.

4.   Explain that you are calling to provide information the DM requested earlier.

Avoid getting drawn into a detailed explanation of your product or what it costs. To do this, try to remain focused on the overall conceptual level of what it can do for the DM's organization.

When you call, be prepared to suggest to the DM alternate choices of times. This simplifies the scheduling process. It also allows you to group your calls for greater efficiency.

If you're not sure whether you should be meeting with this person or organization, ask questions, and maybe even tell a little more about your product or service than you normally would, as a way of screening out those for whom a face-to-face call would not prove worthwhile.

Chapter 7: Organizing and Learning From Your Phone Calls

Particularly at the start, you're going to spend a good many hours on the phone as you get your selling effort rolling. Phone time getting appointments is time well-spent, as one confirmed appointment is a lot better than wasting a day ,driving in circles and sitting in reception areas trying to find someone who's in the office with time to hear you out.

The phone work will get easier and quicker as you refine your approach, but at the start you are climbing up several steep learning curves, all at the same time: you are learning,

- How to convey your message quickly and persuasively on the phone;

- What "hot-buttons" work for your product or service (or how to adapt your product or service so it does have hot-buttons: after all, what you learn from your early marketing efforts may send you back to the drawing board to redesign your product, or may force you to modify your marketing approach);

- How to organize yourself and the data you get from prospects so you can travel efficiently through your territory.

In this chapter, we address the first of these learning curves: that is, improving your telephone technique. The second type of learning -- adapting from customer feedback -- is up to you, as only you know your product and market. We'll be covering that the third learning curve -- organizing and managing yourself as a sales person -- later in this book.

Checklist for listening to yourself

When you begin phoning for appointments, keep a small tape recorder on your desk, and record yourself as you make your calls for appointments.

Do not tape the other person's side of the call, as in many jurisdictions it is illegal to tape someone else on the phone unless you tell them and get their permission . . . and that would certainly distract from your selling message. But so far as I know, there is no law against taping yourself. (Warning: you may not like what you hear from yourself at first. But stick with it: improvement comes.)

After you hang up, play back your end of the conversation and assess how you sounded. Here's a checklist of things to listen for. Add your own ideas, as well.

1. Overall, did you come across as professional? Enthusiastic? Knowledgeable about your product and the market?

2. Did you sound natural? Did you sound like one human being phoning another, or did you come across like one of those computer-automated phone marketing machines that talk on and on, incapable of listening or varying the discussion?

3. Did you sound as though you were reading from a script? That's not good. (It's a good idea to have an outline of key

talking points in front of you, but a full script is a bad idea, as very few people can read a script and sound natural.)

4. How did your voice sound? For both men and women, the deeper and more resonant the better. When under stress, the voices of both men and women rise and become more shrill. ("Deep" and "resonant" are relative terms. The point is to sound natural and confident.)

5. Could you hear a smile in your voice? Even though the DM can't see you over the phone, she can still hear a smile. The best way is to speak with a smile literally on your face. A smile can't be seen over the phone, but it can be heard. A smile impacts your mood, and shapes the way your voice projects.

6. Was your pronunciation clear? If you found some of the words were mumbled, think what it was like for the stranger on the other end of the line.

7. Were your pace and tempo appropriate? There is a middle ground between being so slow that the other person wishes you'd just get on with it, and so fast it sounds like you're mumbling a script you've said a thousand times before.

Be ready to adjust your rate of speech to the listener. Listen for little things like "Uh huh, yeah, I understand," or "Yeah, yeah, yeah," which are subtle clues to move faster. Be alert also to clues that you may be moving too fast, such as a DM asking you to repeat or explain, or even the kind of silence that indicates the other person is not quite tracking with you.

8. Did you personalize the conversation, so it sounded like a conversation, rather than you "talking at" the other person? Did you use their name a few times to make them feel that you are talking to them personally? Did you use "joint" words like "we" and "our" to convey that you and the DM are sharing the call?

9. Was your choice of language positive? Clear? We'll be looking in more detail about projecting positive expectations through your words. Basically, it is using words like "when we meet," not "if we meet."

Also, be careful about using too much insider jargon, or about being too technical at this point. If you are calling an appropriate Decision Maker, with Authority, Need, and Dollars, she may not know (nor need or want to know) the difference between megabytes, megahertz, and megaphones. A DM is interested in bottom-line effect, and the technical aspects matter only as a means to an end.) You don't want to lose the DM before getting the chance to meet face-to-face to make your case.

10. Did you handle any questions or objections confidently and persuasively?

Keep a record of the questions and objections that come up repeatedly. Figure out the best response for each, outline it on paper, then rehearse it until the words flow smoothly and confidently.

Try to boil your responses down to the minimum number of words that make the point. Remember, time on the phone is precious, and you don't want to get bogged down on "perfect" answers that cause the DM to tune you out.

11. Did you sound persuasive? Were you successful in getting the appointment? Why? If not, why not? What could you have done better?

PART THREE: HELPING THE DECISION MAKER RECOGNIZE A NEED FOR YOUR PRODUCT

The central question we address in this Part: How can I get this Decision Maker excited enough to buy my product or service?

In Part One, we worked through the early steps in the selling process: first researching to locate priority prospects, then finding the key Decision Maker within the organizations you target.

Remember: For our purposes, the "Decision Maker" or Prospect is the person (or team) with positive decision making authority: that is, who has the Authority, Need, and Dollars to say Yes to what you are offering.

In Part Two, we worked through making the first contacts with that DM: phoning for an appointment, getting through the secretarial "Screen," and persuading the DM to meet with you. We also examined how to open that sales call effectively.

Now the preliminaries are out of the way. In this Part Three, we get to the core of the persuasive process. First, we examine some productive ways of opening the face-to-face meeting with the Decision Maker. Then we move on through the various ways of convincing the Decision Maker to sign an order (or take some other kind of buying action, such as agreeing to attend your product demonstration).

Why people buy, and how you can help them want to buy
Before getting to the how-to, we need to put it into perspective: Why do people buy? More specifically, why would they buy the product or service you are offering?

Organizations, and the Decision Makers within them, buy only when they arrive at solidly "Yes" answers to four fundamental questions:

1. Do we face a need?

We buy if and only if we feel a need. Without the pull of that need, all the bells and whistles, and all the price discounts and special offers, are powerless to bring about the sale.

2. Is that need significant enough to justify our spending some money to fill it?

We all face a variety of needs, more needs than we could ever hope to fill, so only the needs we perceive as truly significant get priority.

Therefore, one of your most important tasks as you sell is to help the potential customer not only become aware of a need that can be filled by your product or service, but also become enthusiastic about filling it. That is, you should work to develop the awareness of need if none exists, or to enhance a need if it is already present in the Decision Maker's awareness.

3. Will this product or service actually fill that need?

Only after the need and its importance are clear to the DM is it appropriate to begin talking about your product and what it can do for the customer. After all, the DM IS NOT interested in buying your product for its own sake. What the potential buyer IS interested in is finding a way of filling the need that now seems important. Your product becomes of interest insofar as it is a useful means to filling that need.

Therefore, to make the sale, you'll need to make the link clear between the specific needs of the customer (as you have explored them together) and the specific ways in which your product can fill those needs. (We'll examine ways of making this linkage clear in Chapter 14.)

4. Will it fill the need better or more cost-effectively than other approaches?

To conclude the sale, you'll need to deal with the issue of cost. But as we'll see, price is rarely as important as you think. What really matters is not what your product costs, so much as its "cost-effectiveness" -- that is, what the customer gets in return for the money spent. The key is to show how the $1.00 spent for your product brings back $1.01, or, even better $1.25. (We'll examine ways of accomplishing this in Chapter 15.)

These "other approaches" are, basically, your competition. The competition may take the form of other vendors like yourself. Or the "competition" may be the tendency to do nothing, and hence continue the status quo.

As a general strategy it's best to ignore the competition when you're speaking with the Decision Maker until the DM raises these other possibilities through a question or objection. Then you can distinguish your approach from the competing approaches, showing why yours is best.

The core of the selling process, then, is guiding the Decision Maker in looking at the situation to determine whether Yes answers are appropriate to these four questions. "Yes" to these four should lead naturally to "Yes" to the overall question of "Should we buy?"

In this Part Three, we look at ways of helping the DM arrive at positive answers to the first two of these questions:

1. Do we face a need?

2. Is that need significant enough to justify our spending some money to fill it?

Part Four will focus on the two remaining questions.

Chapter 8: Opening the Face-To-Face Meeting with the Decision Maker

To this point, our focus has been on locating the appropriate Decision Maker, and on convincing that DM to meet with you. Now we skip ahead in time to the day of your first meeting with the Decision Maker.

It's a good idea to confirm that the meeting is still on before setting out on the journey to the DM's office. A quick phone call reminds the DM of the meeting, and ensures that she'll be there when you arrive. If not, you can reschedule.

Your call to confirm has a second benefit: it subtly projects that you value your time. That kind of self-confidence conveys to the DM that you and your product are worth hearing about.

When to make this confirming call? If you appointment is set for the morning, confirm it the afternoon before. Otherwise, if it's afternoon or late morning, check in with a call that morning.

- *"This is Jeremy Triplett with QMS Associates. I'm calling to confirm my appointment with Ms. Hardy at two-thirty today. Is that still on schedule? Good. I'll be there for two-thirty this afternoon."*

When you make this call to confirm, ask to speak the DM's secretary (whose name you should already know.) There's no need to disturb the DM herself when you confirm. The secretary either keeps the DM's appointment book, or will check it for you.

Picking up clues when you're in the outer office

When you arrive, give the receptionist or secretary your business card, and say that the DM is expecting you at this time. (Business cards are cheap advertising; keep a supply in the pocket of your jacket where you can reach them easily.)

As you wait, scan the office for clues that may help you shape your sales message:

- Take a quick look at any corporate publications you find in the reception area, such as internal newsletters, capability statements or brochures, annual reports, or scrapbooks of news clippings. These often suggest what themes are important there this year. It may be productive to echo them in your presentation.

- Although your earlier research prior to contacting the Decision Maker should have turned up information on these themes, it's still a good idea to check over the data available on-site. What you find in this senior person's waiting area may be a lot more informative than what you saw out in the general reception area.

- Be attuned to the messages conveyed by the office furnishings and tone. For instance, if the furniture looks like World War II salvage, then consider making "economy" and "cost savings" key words in your presentation. Conversely, a sleek, high-tech office with the latest in equipment may suggest that you stress how up-to-date, even ahead of the wave, your work or product is.

When and how to use business cards, brochures, and other sales aids

It's a good idea to give the DM another business card as you shake hands. That ensures that she has your name and your firm's name in front of her as you talk, and isn't distracted with trying to remember it.

But *do not* give either the DM (or secretary/receptionist) any of your brochures or written materials at this point. If you do, the chances are that the DM will spend the meeting reading through them, and you'll find yourself talking to the top of a head bent over reading your literature.

The most effective use of brochures and sales literature is to integrate them as selling tools in the body of your presentation.

Your opening: echo the hot-button that worked on the phone

In your earlier phone contact with the Decision Maker, you had only a few seconds to trigger interest, and convince her to invest time in meeting with you.

But you can't take for granted that this interest will carry over from that phone conversation until today's meeting. In the days since then, she may have fielded hundreds of other calls, and now may have only a vague memory of who you are, and why it seemed a good idea to invest time in meeting with you.

Pressed now with other concerns, she may be looking for a reason to end it quickly and get on to what seem to be more important matters.

For that reason, it's good practice to spend a few moments at the start recapturing her previous interest, and setting the stage for a successful call. Here's how:

1. Review the interest-generating statement you used during the phone conversation.

What you say now should not be a word-for-word repeat of your phone message, but rather should echo the essence of that conversation as a brief reminder of the hot buttons that captured interest earlier. But be brief. This should normally not take more than a couple of sentences:

- *"As I mentioned in our phone conversation last week ..."*

2. If appropriate, cite a BRIEF success story to heighten interest.

Here's a model you can adapt to fit your situation:

- *"We've recently been able to help a number of other engineering firms in this area. For example, we saved Brown and Hennessey nearly a thousand dollars per month in clerical costs. Stone and Feeney were about to hire an additional secretary, but the productivity gains we developed made that unnecessary -- again, a very large savings in direct salary, benefits, and even office space.*

- *"It's that kind of experience that makes me confident we can be equally helpful to you, so I'd like to begin by asking a few questions to determine where we might best be able to help your organization."*

Be prepared for possible last-minute hesitations

Sometimes, at about this point at the start of the call, the DM may raise objections like these:

"You'd be wasting your time."

"I've decided I'm not interested."

"My job is to practice law, and I leave decisions about systems to my office manager."

"We already investigated this idea, and decided it's not right for us."

"We don't have any money."

Respond to last-minute hesitations in the same way you do for other objections. In later chapters in this book. we introduce the basic model for responding to questions and objections, examine the specifics of dealing with "early" objections like these.

Whether and when to use "Ice-Breakers"
The approach recommended here is direct and down-to-business: introduce yourself, refresh the Decision Maker's recollection of why she agreed to see you, then, if appropriate, briefly cite a relevant success story.

But you should be aware that there is another school of thought on how to open the sales call. Some sales people prefer to open with "ice-breakers," hoping to build rapport before getting down to business. Thus they might first spend some time chatting about the weather or traffic, or about the golf or fishing trophies they see on the wall.

But project yourself into the DM's shoes, and you'll probably conclude -- with me -- that ice-breakers are not a good idea. The DM invited you for a business purpose, not a social call. Given today's pace of work, few have time to kill on small-talk with strangers.

Besides, if you open the call by talking about golf or trivia, you come across as someone who's not very serious about business. Even worse, you may be perceived as manipulative. The DM knows why you are there, and will appreciate your getting on with things, and not wasting valuable business time.

Still, there are some circumstances, and some parts of the country, where ice-breakers are appropriate. For example, if you already know the DM from another context -- perhaps from a church, civic, or professional organization, or from passing on the golf course -- a few words are in order.

Similarly, in some locales, (especially smaller towns where the pace is slower and people tend to be more interested in others), a little socializing may be appropriate at the start of the call.

If you do choose to open with ice-breakers, be alert to signals that the DM is ready to get to business. Often a shift in the chair from a relaxed to an upright position indicates the shift in interest. Another signal may be a change in expression as the welcoming smile shifts to a more formal expression.

For more guidance on reading the DM's non-verbal signals, see the later chapter: Sending and Receiving Non-Verbal Messages.

Summary

Get to the DM's office early enough, so that you have time to get a sense of the themes that are important in that organization this year.

Don't take for granted that the DM still recalls why she agreed to meet. Spend a few moments introducing yourself, and BRIEFLY recapturing interest. Approaches include,

1. Reviewing the interest-generating statement you used during the phone conversation.

2. Citing a BRIEF success story to heighten interest.

Be prepared to respond to any last-minute reluctance to meet with you.

Normally avoid wasting time at the start with ice-breakers. Unless there is a sound reason --- such as a personal acquaintanceship with the DM, or the custom of the region --- respect the DM's time and get on with the purpose of your call.

Chapter 9: Developing and Enhancing the Decision Maker's Awareness of a Need

As we examined in the overview to this Part, organizations, and the Decision Makers within them, buy only when they arrive, consciously or sub-consciously, at solidly Yes answers to four questions.

1. Do we face a need?

2. Is that need significant enough to justify our spending some money to fill it?

3. Will this product or service actually fill that need?

4. Will it fill the need better or more cost-effectively than other approaches?

In this chapter, we examine the impact of the first two of these questions, which focus on spotting needs, and how significant those needs are to the Prospect. Basically, people (organizations) only buy if they feel a need, and if that need is significant.

Typically, at the start of the sales process, the Prospect will not feel a strong sense of need. The status quo may not be perfect, but it's comfortable, and may seem adequate. Thus to make the sale you will usually either help *create* (from scratch) or *enhance* (make stronger) a sense of a need.

In some cases, the Decision Maker will already be aware of the need. But caution: even if the DM and others in the organization already acknowledge the need, it's nonetheless good practice to take the time to strengthen that awareness of need in order to increase their readiness for what you offer. One way is to DM understand what those *unfilled needs are costing, both directly and indirectly.*

In both developing and enhancing the awareness of need, three main approaches are generally helpful. That is, you can . . .

1. Let your product (or work sample) *speak for itself.*

Advantages: There are products that can easily sell themselves, at least if the conditions are right. Ice cream cones and convertibles on sunny spring days fit into this category, because they create their own sense of "need" -- to see them is to want them. Similarly, if your product (or service) has the good fortune of arriving in a hot market at the right time, it can also sell itself.

Disadvantages: If you rely on the product to sell itself, you risk finding yourself trapped on a one-way corridor to the exit if the DM's awareness of the need does not blossom of its own accord when he sees your product.

I think of this approach as the "Drop it on their desk and hope they like it."

If there's no immediate recognition of need, or if the DM fails to immediately make the connection between the need as he perceives it and how your product can fill that need, then you face the DM's response, "Looks nice. Great idea. But so what?" If you encounter that kind of block, it's difficult to get selling momentum going again.

In short, relying on your product or service to sell itself MAY work, but it's a risky strategy. Besides, if it doesn't immediately "click" with the DM, you don't have a foundation to support other attempts. The basic difficulty in expecting the product or service to do your selling for you is that the DM lacks a mental framework for seeing it in overall context. That is, he sees a solution (your product), but just why he needs that solution may not be apparent.

You may wonder: If the start of the call is not the time to show your product, then when *is* the right time? Basically, *after the need for it has been established.* First, get the DM aware of a need, and looking for a way of filling that need. Then show how your product fits that need. (We look at this in Part Four.)

2. Tell the client about the need.

Advantages: If the DM is open to it, and if done skillfully, this can be a very efficient way of getting to the core of your selling message. You can move more directly into presenting your solution, with no further preliminaries.

Disadvantages: If not done with skill, then you risk antagonizing the DM, or bringing out a defensiveness that blocks further progress. People -- even chief executives -- don't like being told that things are less than perfect in their area of responsibility. They may become defensive and stop listening to what else you're saying.

Clearly, statements such as, "You really need the software I sell because your billing department is a mess," tend to be too direct, and so are likely only to antagonize the DM and make him defensive and unwilling to listen further.

However, if you put these needs in context, or if you manage to depersonalize or generalize them, you may be able to speak of problems and resulting needs without raising defensive hackles and making the DM feel put on the spot. One way is to speak in general terms, without pointing the finger at this organization or DM. For example:

- *"We find that many of our clients have had difficulties in (fill in according to your situation)"*

- *Or, "It often happens that start-up small business ventures find themselves handicapped by (fill in, according to the need your product or service fills)."*

Another approach that can allow you to speak directly of problems and needs without making the DM defensive is to use an "informational" presentation.

For example, a consultant specializing in helping firms comply with government regulations might open sales calls with a presentation overviewing the area, pointing out how complex the area is, and how costly a failure to comply can be. To make her points more clearly -- without seeming to point fingers at individuals -- she could "show-and-tell," using visuals such as news clippings on the fines and civil judgments paid by firms that failed to comply. She could then go on to cite the success stories of other clients she has helped. (Caution: be sure to get clearance from those other clients before citing them by name.)

3. Ask the right questions, so the DM tells you of the need.

The easiest time to sell something is immediately after the DM has told you why she needs it -- and maybe even told you how your product will help pay for itself in other savings.

There is little you can say to compare in power and credibility with having the DM tell you of the need and implications in her own words. Besides, if you nudge the discussion in the right direction, the DM will not only tell you of the need, but will also tell you of the dollars-and-cents reasons why it makes sound business sense for the organization to fill that need (and hence buy your product or service) NOW.

Sound too good to be true? Actually, getting the DM to do this for you doesn't take magic or sorcery -- simply the patience to listen well . . . and the knack of asking the right questions.

Sometimes you may not even need to prompt with questions, particularly if the prospect invited you to come in and make a presentation. In that happy situation, the DM is likely already aware of a need, and is primed for a way of filling it. Thus all you may need to do is listen to the DM, and sort through the data presented to find the facts that make your case for you.

More often, though, you'll need to take an active role by guiding the DM through a sequenced series of questions. (We'll examine some how-to ideas for those questions in the next Chapter.)

Disadvantages: Working through the question-and-answer dialogue takes time. Thus it may not be practical in selling small-ticket items. Similarly, some Decision Makers may be too rushed or too impatient to allow you the time to ask all the questions you would like. Thus you must be ready to ask the right questions, but also flexible enough so you can switch to another approach, if necessary.

This approach, based on asking savvy questions, is a key part of what is termed *Consultative Selling*. Consultants ask savvy questions to isolate needs and point the way to appropriate solutions, and smart sales people model on that approach.

Asking the smart questions: The "Consultative Selling Wedge"

In your question-and-answer dialogue with the DM, you have two key objectives to accomplish. First, to educate yourself about the problem and resulting needs.

Second -- no less important -- to "bring the client with you" through your analytical process. You may already be virtually certain, from your experience with other clients, what the DM's answers are likely to be. From that, the needs are clear . . . but typically clear only to you.

To make sure that the DM is mentally "tracking" with you through all the steps of the process, it's important to ask all the questions, and work together through each mental step. Some questions and answers may seem so obvious as hardly to be worth mentioning. But keep in mind that you have been through this analysis before, while it's all new to the Decision Maker.

By asking the questions, you get the DM talking -- and hence thinking with fresh perspective. Once the DM has put into her own words sound reasons in favor of your proposal, you can then echo those words later as "authority" supporting your case. What the DM tells you about the need, and the implications flowing from it, is going to carry far more weight than anything you could say.

Besides, even though you may be totally confident that you know what the answers are going to be, you may be surprised by the responses of this unique Decision Maker and organization.

Useful question-and-answer dialogues of the kind that lead to sales don't often happen by chance. It helps to work systematically through a well-planned sequence of questions that brings out the facts of the situation, logically leading to the conclusions you seek.

We address the how-to of selling by asking the right questions in the following chapters.

Summary

If you are to make the sale, the Decision Maker must, **first**, be aware that a need exists; **second**, be convinced that the need is significant enough to justify spending money to fill; and, **third**, be confident that what you propose is the best way of filling that need;

Three main strategies for helping the Prospect recognize the need and its significance:

1. Let your product speak for itself. Sometimes just showing what you have, or samples of its output, are all that it takes to create the sense of need, and hence make the sale. But these are relatively rare cases. If the product alone doesn't do it, then you may be stranded with no way of getting the sale going.

2. Tell the client of the need they face. Sometimes this works. But sometimes it antagonizes and creates a defensiveness that blocks progress.

3. Ask the right questions, and so lead the customer to tell you of the need. This seems to take longer than these first two methods. But getting the customer talking is usually a far more productive selling approach, as the DM develops a real sense of the situation, and a sense of "ownership" of the solution. (Selling by asking the right questions is a central part of what is termed "consultative selling.")

Chapter 10: Selling By Asking Questions: The "Selling Wedge"

In the previous chapter, we examined the three main ways of developing or enhancing the Decision Maker's awareness of the needs which you can fill: you can show, tell, or ask.

1. *Show* the product (or samples), and hope it sells itself.

2. *Tell* the client of the needs they face.

3. *Ask* the right questions, so the client tells you of the need and its significance.

Approaches 1 (show) and 2 (tell), as we saw, carry significant disadvantages. When using them, you're basically "selling at" the Decision Maker -- that is, "pushing your product." The sales call can easily degenerate into a competition pitting you and your product against the customer.

By speaking of your product before really listening to the DM's needs, you subtly convey that you put your own interests first, ahead of those of the customer. You *may* get the sale. But then again you may *antagonize* the customer who resents being "sold."

The third approach—asking savvy questions--avoids those difficulties. By asking the DM to tell you about the general situation, and then about the needs that have developed, you begin a dialogue.

From this dialogue will come a shared awareness of the facts behind the problem, as well as a shared sense of "ownership" of the solution that results.

Beyond that, the Prospect will develop a sense of trust in you, as well as confidence both in your shared diagnosis of the problem and of the solution you propose.

As helpful as that question-answer dialogue usually is both to you and the customer, there is nothing magical about it. What makes it work are basic common-sense questions that progress from broad context to target in on specific needs.

The pattern of the questions you ask in developing or enhancing need resemble a wedge:

Broad overview questions at the start.

Focusing-in questions to help the Prospect become aware of what needs exist.

Value questions to lead the Prospect to think about and put into words and dollars the value of filling those needs.

Keep that concept of the wedge in mind as it's a helpful mental framework for structuring the questions. We'll refer to that as the "Consultative Selling Wedge."

Let's look in more depth at each of those three types of questions within the Consultative Selling Wedge.

Overview questions

At this stage, you are looking for an overall "map" of broad areas such as the organization and its work flow. You are also looking for the first indications of what potential problem areas may be worth probing in more detail. (What these problem areas are will depend on what your product is.)

Useful Overview Questions develop both background facts, as well as a sense of context. They are usually open-ended, so the person has considerable freedom and scope in responding. The responses should provide you an overall "map" of the terrain.

Here's a model script to adapt for opening the sales call and transitioning into the questions that will lead the customer to talk of needs. (It fits at the very start of the call, as soon as you have settled into your chair.)

- *"As I mentioned on the phone, I've been able to help a number of other small manufacturers in the area to increase productivity -- on average by 10%. I'm here because I believe I can do the same for your firm. To help me better target my presentation to your actual needs, perhaps you could give me a brief overview of how you presently handle the match between orders and output."*

In your opening, you can narrow the question by reflecting what you have already learned, as in, *"My particular focus is on how you _____."*

Generally, the DM's overview will slow within a couple of minutes. Depending on whether you have enough promising leads, you can either extend the overview by asking another broad question, or can target in to follow up on loose threads.

Caution: don't be too quick to cut off the overview being given by the Prospect. It may be tempting to listen to just enough, then jump into a discussion of what you "know" are the needs the customer faces, and the ways your product or service can help.

But if you skip to talking of solutions before establishing with the DM a shared understanding of the problem, you will tend to lose the DM's confidence, as you are taking mental leaps that he does not follow.

Typically, if you resist that temptation to jump in, and instead let the DM roll, you will find that several different potential need areas may emerge, as may a number of different "avenues" to one broad need.

For instance, as you listen, you might hear one loose thread relating to the need to speed up a work process in the DM's operation, another relating to excessive labor costs, and a third that might come at the need from the viewpoint of how the client could improve service to their own customers. All three may offer you different approaches for showing how your product can fill the need.

Other typical Overview Questions: "What does your unit do here? Can you give me an overview of your operation?"

"Focusing-in" questions

As the DM gives you that overview, listen for loose threads that may lead to needs you can fill.

With experience, you will develop a sense of the common types of loose threads relevant to your product or service. Even more importantly, with experience you will develop an intuitive sense, or "nose," for relevant trouble areas, even in novel areas of opportunity.

Concentrate on each area in turn. As you follow up each area, "focus-in" more closely with your questions to explore whether a problem does in fact exist.

In going back to follow up on a loose thread, you can say something on the order of "You mentioned that you were experiencing a bottleneck in shipping. Can you tell me more about that?"

What you are looking for here is the DM's statement of facts that provide evidence of the need for your product. Precisely what form this evidences take will depend on what your product is, and what it does to help users. For example, if your product is a software package that simplifies tracking items and consolidating paperwork, then you would listen for hints that the difficulties relate to these areas.

Make note of this evidences, either mentally or on paper. Try to capture the DM's actual words and data, as you will want to echo these later. There is no better "authority" than the DM's statements. For example, suppose the DM talks of the need to hire temporary workers one week each month in order to get a certain report out. Hold onto the cost figures for use later (and be attuned to both direct costs (salaries) and indirect costs (such as training each month's team of temporaries).

Later, in making the point that your software package can pay for itself by saving those expenses: *"You said that ____. We can help you there, since ____."*

So far as possible, let the DM roll, telling of the situation in her own words. You may need to probe with additional questions either to get the details you need, or to keep the DM on-track. But the tone should be that of a conversation, not an interrogation: try to minimize your interruptions.

Not every "loose thread" will lead to a need you can fill. Some will turn out to be dead ends as far as evidencing the need for your product or service. If that's the case, let it go, and ask about another thread. *"You also mentioned ____ . Can we talk about that for a moment?"*

If a thread continues to look promising, stay with it. Probe with more questions if necessary in order to get the DM stating clearly why that need is worth filling. Just how significant that need is, and how your product can fill it, may be perfectly obvious to you. But keep in mind that you are an expert on your product and its uses. The DM does not have that kind of familiarity. Thus, if you are to make the sale, it's important for the DM to "feel" that need as vividly as possible.

One way, as we examined earlier, would be to tell the DM of the need and its significance. But telling has its disadvantages: basically, Decision Makers discount what sales people tell them.

That's why it's usually better to continue asking the questions that get the DM to tell you, in his own words, what that unfilled need means: what is it costing while it remains unfilled? These "costs," depending on the situation, may be in dollars, inconvenience, distractions, and the like.

Don't stop listening after just one loose thread. When you have established one clear need for your product, it's tempting to skip to showing just how it can fill those needs. However, the more needs exist that you can fill, the better will be your chances of making the sale. Once the first need is established, I tuck it away in my head and move on to establishing the second and third needs. Only after I have all or most of the needs do I begin to show how my service can fill the most important of those needs. (The third or fifth need may be the most powerful, from a selling perspective.)

Other typical "Focusing-in" questions include, "You mentioned earlier that you sometimes experienced bottlenecks when the SMG section got overloaded. When might that happen? How often does it occur?"

Value questions

These final questions in the series should test the significance of the problem (or need area), and develop an awareness of the consequences.

The purpose of these final questions is to get the prospect to put into his own words how useful it would be to the organization to fill the need that you have been exploring through your questions.

Once the Decision Maker articulates just how valuable it would be to fill the need, you can later quote this back to him as a sound justification supporting your recommended solution. ("As you said earlier, Ms. Swenson, your operation is having difficulties with ____ .")

At this stage, you would also be asking other specific testing questions on the dollar value of filling the need, as that information will be valuable in a later step, when you show the value of installing your proposal. (We examine the methods for establishing value in Chapters 14 and 15.)

Other typical "Value" questions: "Suppose you were able to eliminate the weekly backups in the SMG section -- how would that affect the rest of the assembly line? What are these delays costing you? You said that as a result of the bottlenecks you sometimes have to run another shift on overtime on the weekend -- what does that cost? How is the morale holding up of the employees who have to come in on Saturdays?"

Model Consulting Sales Wedge Dialogue

Here's a shortened version of the questions as they might transpire if I were to make a call to sell sales training workshops based on this book.

Q: (This is an Overview Question). "I notice that a lot of the machines here in the plant are shut down. Are they not in use, or are the workers on break?"

A: "They're not in use now. Things are a little slow here these days."

Q: (Another Overview Question.) "May I ask what percentage of capacity you're running at now?"

A: "Sixty-five percent."

Q: (Focusing-in Question.) "If you're only at 65%, then a lot of capacity must be sitting idle. Is that because sales are below what they should be?"

A: "We're very disappointed in our sales."

Q: (Focusing-in.) "How large is your sales staff? What level of experience?"

A: "Right now just four people. We're looking for a couple more. Actually, to tell the truth, we probably should just go ahead and replace the people we have -- except that the new ones would have even less experience."

Q: (Focusing-in.) "Can you tell me some more about the difficulties your sales people are having?"

A: "Frankly, I'm not really sure what the problem is. We have a good product, and there's a real need for it. But the sales force just doesn't seem to know how to find the right prospects, or how to get orders from those they do find."

Q: (Value.) "You mentioned that the plant is operating at only 65% of its potential capacity. What would the effect be on your bottom line if sales went up enough to get up to 70% capacity? To 75%? To 80%?"

A: "Right now, the way things are, we're losing money every day. If we could get up to 70%, we'd begin to break even. At 80%, we'd have to add some staff, but we'd be making money hand-over-fist."

Cycle back through the wedge to develop additional needs

After you've worked through the Wedge question sequence of Overview, then Focusing-in, then Value to establish the first potential customer Need, then you can recycle back to the Wedge to pick up on another clue and carry it through to a second area of Need, and then a third, and so forth.

In recycling for these additional needs, you won't necessarily need to begin at the start with another Overview. Instead, you can cut back to something the DM said, as in, *"You mentioned also that _____. I'd like to explore that for a moment. Does it ever happen that _____ ?"*

Summary

While you could let the product speak for itself to do your selling, or come straight-out and tell the client of the need they face for your product, these methods can backfire and alienate the customer.

It's usually better to bring the Decision Maker in as a partner in solving the problem by asking the right questions. These questions get the prospect thinking in a fresh way about the situation, and, if there is a need for your product, putting into his or her own words the indictors that prove that need, as well as the value of filling that need.

The "Consultative Selling Wedge" provides a useful structure for this kind of productive dialogue. Basically, ask common-sense questions that go from the broad situation to target specific needs.

Overview questions

Core Overview Question: What relevant tasks or activities are performed here?

Typical/sample Overview questions: What does your unit do? Can you give me an overview of the operation?

Focusing-in questions

Core Focusing-in Question: What obstacles/ difficulties/ bottlenecks are arising here?

Sample Focusing-in questions: You mentioned earlier that sometimes things go wrong. When? How often? Any idea why?

Value questions

Core Value Question: What direct and indirect costs result from that unfilled Need? What other effects result?

Typical Value Questions: What is this costing you -- directly, or out-of-pocket? Any indirect effects, such as lowered morale, customer dissatisfaction?

Some "if-all-else-fails" probing questions

If I'm in a sales call, and find my usual question sequence doesn't seem to be pulling out any possibilities, I may fall back on somewhat whimsical, very open-ended questions like these. My aim is to get a dialog going about needs..

- If I could do one thing for your organization as it is today, what would that one thing be?

- If I happened to have a magic solution in my briefcase for your most pressing need right now, what form would it take? Can you describe it for me? Can you describe what it would do for you? Why that particular need?

These are only suggestions to get you started. If the sales call seems to be dead-ended, you have little to lose, so can afford to be a little whimsical in approach.

Don't hesitate to laugh a little as you ask about magic solutions," as that may open the DM to get into the what-if nature of the exercise.

Chapter 11: Matching the Question Type to the Situation

The questions you ask are like seeds. It's crucial to give them time to grow. After you ask, be silent, even if it means letting the silence hang in the air. That gives the Decision Maker time to think and respond.

Though you ask questions here at this stage of the call, it should never come across as an interrogation. In the ideal case, you ask just one or a few questions to signal direction, then let the DM tell the story in her own words.

Ask a question, then let it "grow" in the silence and listen closely to the response. Ask another question only if you must. In some cases, you'll need to rephrase the question so it's clearer, or to focus the DM's response so it's more on target. But those are exceptions. As a rule, once you've asked the question, bite your tongue and let the DM talk.

There are other good reasons to ask fewer questions and allow more silence: constant interruptions to ask new questions may irritate the DM. Besides, if you let the DM go on at her own pace, and in the general direction she thinks best, you may find other potential needs opening up in ways that you wouldn't have anticipated.

Above all, don't be so busy asking questions (and thinking of what your next questions will be) that you neglect to listen to the answers you do get.

Important: Why you should not ask the Prospect about "problems"

It's true that you're meeting with the Prospect in order to find problems that your product can solve.

But do not ask about "problems," because good managers do not have problems.

Or at least they won't *admit* to any problems in their area. After all, eliminating problems is part of their job as manager, and to admit that problems can exist is about the same as admitting they haven't been doing their job well.

Besides, problems are often not recognized as problems. Instead, situations may be taken for granted, because they have always been part of the environment, and so are assumed to be just a fact of life, not something that can be rectified or improved.

To get around this bind, find other words that you can use in place of "problem," as you get the DM to discuss the situation. The word "needs" doesn't carry the emotional baggage for managers that "problems" does, and you can usually ask, "What needs are you facing here?" without pushing the DM into denial.

Other helpful words include "difficulties," "bottlenecks," and "obstacles." Or you might speak of "areas needing improvement." There may be still other terms particularly relevant to your product or industry.

In some cases, it's helpful to approach from the opposite direction: that is, instead of focusing on the negative side (the needs), ask about the positive aspect, such as "goals," "desires," "plans," "proposed improvements," and the like.

Other ways the questions help your marketing

We're emphasizing asking questions to get the DM talking about needs. But there is another way in which the questions and answers help: as you work with the DM, her responses may give you very helpful product and market research.

The DM's responses can tell you,

- about new products that you could develop, suggested by this prospect's special needs;

- about uses for your product that hadn't occurred to you;

- ways in which your existing product or service can be modified or expanded to fit needs you had been unaware of.

The DM may even give you helpful advice on your product or your marketing approach. This advice may come as advice, or may come in the form of questions, comments, or objections.

When Hewlett-Packard decided to shift one division from defense work to entering the growing market for professional video equipment, it listened to the customer in a big way. As one H-P manager put it in *Fortune*, "We did no formal training. We bought people airline tickets and books and sent them out to spend a lot of time with customers. They left as microwave engineers and came back as video engineers."

The point is that if Hewlett-Packard can learn from customers' comments and questions, so can small entrepreneurs.

Basic question types and their uses

Keep in mind that there are three main types of questions:

Open-ended questions. Example: "What do you know about asking questions?"

Closed-ended questions. Example: "In what situations would you use questions as selling tools?"

Yes-No questions. Example: "Do you think you ask enough questions?"

"Open-ended questions," as the name implies, give the person who's asked wide-open range within which to respond. In the first example above, notice how wide a scope is provided by the question, "What do you know about asking questions?" The other person has the freedom to answer with very little, or to give a lecture on more than you'd ever want to know.

"Closed-ended" or "targeted" questions narrow the range of response. You can use them either to collect information (the normal use of questions), or you can use them "Socratically," asking the question to get the other person thinking about something they might not have, or in a new way. For example, I might have asked "In what situations would you use questions as selling tools?" not because I wanted to hear the response, but instead as a subtle way of making the other person realize that questions could be used for non-traditional purposes, such as selling.

"Yes-no" questions are even narrower: if the other person responds to the question as you asked it, the only reasonable responses are either "Yes," or "No." (With perhaps "I don't know," and "Maybe" as possibilities.)

For your purposes in selling, it's not particularly important to remember the names or the definitions of the three types. But it IS important that you keep aware of the different forms of questions that are available, and the particular and the particular uses of each.

Ask Open-ended questions when you want to get the other person talking. These questions give a lot of freedom, and, in answering them, the person has the scope to go wherever he thinks is important. In selling, you would ask Open-ended questions early-on with the DM when you are still learning your way around, and want to get the DM to provide you a "map" of the operation, as well as some broad areas of potential need.

Ask "Closed-ended" or "Targeted" questions once you have a sense of the terrain, and want to focus in on particular areas of interest. Thus you might ask Open-ended questions at the start of the meeting to get a sense of the DM's operation, then zero in on the details of what you expect will be areas of need for your product, asking Closed-ended questions to draw out the details you need.

Ask "Yes-No" questions to pin down specific facts, or to check your understanding of what the DM has said: "If I understood correctly, you said that _____ . Is that correct?"

Keep these three question types in mind as we move on to take another closer look at the Selling Wedge, introduced in the previous chapter. You will be using these three question types -- particularly Open-ended and Closed-ended -- within the framework of the Consultative Selling Wedge, which we'll focus on in the next Chapter.

Chapter 12: The Consultative Selling Wedge: How-To Checklist

It takes a while to acquire the knack of selling by asking questions. The core of the Consultative Selling Wedge approach is simple in concept: ask from general to particular, bringing the DM with you as you analyze the situation and find needs that you can fill.

But it takes practice to come up with the right questions. It's helpful to do some homework before meeting with your first prospects. Think through in advance some of the questions to ask at each stage, so you have a "mental map" to guide you when you're face-to-face with a Decision Maker.

The checklist below guides you in developing questions useful with the Selling Wedge. You'll find model questions appropriate to each level of the Wedge. Adapt them to your particular product or service or selling situation, and jot your own questions in the space provided as a reference for the future.

General rules

In the Overview phase, ask mostly Open-ended questions to get the DM talking.

As you get to the Focusing-in and Value phases, ask fewer Open-ended and more Closed-ended questions.

Use Yes-No questions only when you need to pin down a specific fact. (Yes-No questions tend to close off the discussion.)

As you ask your questions, keep it a conversation, not an interrogation. Let the prospect feel that you want to learn all you can about the situation, so you can help, NOT that you are there to cross-examine.

Caution: Be sensitive to the possibility that the DM may not want to answer some of your questions for reasons of security or competitive advantage. For example, he may be concerned that your questions are getting too close to proprietary information that he doesn't want known outside the company. (These sensitive areas might include work-procedures, how sales have been going lately, how heavily they are staffed in certain areas, production costs, potential profitability, and the like.)

Be alert to the kind of signals that might tell you that you are probing sensitive areas. Those signals may include unconscious nonverbal cues, such as facial expressions, sudden reluctance to make eye contact, physical closing up or drawing away from you.

If you encounter this reluctance, suggest something like this:

"I sense that we have moved into an area in which some confidential information is involved, and I respect that. Would it be reasonable, for purposes of illustrating the cost-saving potential of my product, to suggest that a typical hourly cost might be $____? If so, then we can use that, and you can plug in your own actual figures at your convenience. Otherwise, would you like to suggest a hypothetical figure to use?"

Typical Overview Questions

I'd appreciate a quick overview of your operation, as it relates to (area covered by my product, service).

Alternately, What kind of work goes on here? I know you're part of Amalgamated Airlines' data processing department, but I'm not clear yet on how this unit fits into the overall flow.

What are the key tasks performed here? What are the most important work outputs or products?

How many people work in this unit? What kind of job titles? (If relevant)

Where does the work output of this unit go? Who depends on it, such as other parts of this organization, outside customers, etc.?

Alternately, if you're already generally familiar with the operation, or industry: I notice that (whatever is relevant to a need for your product or service) Why is that?

What upgrades or improvements do you have planned for this year?

How do the organization's objectives for the year impact on your unit? With what effect?

Typical "Focusing-in" Questions
Looking at the present situation, and looking ahead to the future, what do you perceive to be your important needs?

Do you ever have any difficulties with (fill in, appropriate to the needs filled by your product or service)? (If necessary, amplify what you meant by "difficulties" in a way that is relevant to the needs filled by your product or service. Difficulties might include delays, low quality, crises, or whatever is appropriate in a way your product or service can help.)

If "difficulties" does not ring a bell with the DM, ask instead, Do any "bottlenecks" or "obstacles ever arise? With what effect?"

If these difficulties/bottlenecks/obstacles occur, what is the result?

About how often do these difficulties occur? Is there any particular pattern? Are there any times when the difficulties have special impact?

How does that affect your operation? Other parts of the organization?

What impact do these difficulties have on your customers or clients? How significant is that to them?

Would it help you if you could (fill in whatever way the product or service can assist)?

Useful with the right kind of prospect at the right time: Suppose you could have one wish granted in relation to that difficulty, what would be it be? (But before asking, be reasonably sure it will relate to your product or service.)

Alternately, if appropriate: What areas have you investigated or attempted to improve upon in the past? Why there? With what effect?

Typical "Value" Questions

When these kinds of difficulties arise, what does it cost?

- Direct costs, such as wasted time, materials?

- Indirect costs, such as throwing work schedules off?

- Costs to other units of this organization?

When the difficulties arise, what is the impact on your clients or customers? Does that cost them out-of-pocket? Has it ever resulted in your losing good customers? How often? With what dollar effect to you?

Suppose I could (fill in what your product or service might do to help the situation)? How would that help you? In terms of dollars, what effect would that have?

If you could eliminate the impact of that difficulty, what would it be worth to you? Alternately, If you could reduce the impact by, for example (10% or 30% etc.) what would it be worth?

To a Decision Maker who says something like, "It would be worth a lot," Can you translate that to an estimate of dollars and cents?

What about direct savings, such as the cost of labor and materials saved? What kind of dollars would this translate to?

- What about indirect savings, such as the dollar value of avoiding getting off-schedule?

- What about the real-dollar effect with customers and clients, such as maintaining their good will, and a reputation for delivering on-time? What about the dollar effect if you can avoid losing good customers?

Chapter 13: Selling By Asking Questions: Modeling the Consultative Selling Wedge In Action

In the previous chapters, we examined the how-to of using the Consultative Selling Wedge as a selling tool.

In this chapter, we'll see the Wedge in action in a typical dialogue between a customer and a sales person. This dialogue between a Sales Person (here SP), and a Decision Maker (DM) will help you get a sense of how the questions in the wedge sequence fit together into a conversational flow.

Notice how in practice the three types of questions tend to flow together in a natural, conversational way. When used with skill, the DM does not hear the clanking of gears as the SP shifts from one band of questioning to the next.

In this example, the Sales Person is marketing an improved word-processing system. He is hoping to convince the Decision Maker, here the managing partner in a law firm, to install this equipment in place of an older system that is now in place. This is the seller's first call on this Decision Maker.

Opening statement/Overview questions

SP: "As I mentioned when we spoke on the phone last week, we've been able to help a number of other law firms in the area increase their productivity, and hence their profitability. I'm here because I believe that we can do the same for your firm."

DM: "I hope you can. We can certainly use some help."

SP: "So that I can better direct my explanations to your specific needs, perhaps you could give me a brief overview of your firm? I know you have 22 partners, but how many associates? How large a support staff? What kinds of practice are you involved in? Is the firm sub-divided by specialties?"

DM answers the questions, and the SP follows by asking if there are any plans for expansion. The DM replies, "None beyond normal growth."

Focusing-in questions
SP: "You mentioned that the firm does a lot of trial work for insurance companies. That means that you generate a great deal of paper -- motions, depositions, briefs, and the like. How does all that get typed?"

DM: "Each partner has a secretary. In addition, there is a center to work on large projects."

SP: "Does it ever happen that a crush of typing arrives from several cases at once? Is this ever more than your data input staff can handle easily? What happens then? How do you get the work done and still meet your deadlines? Does that crash effort disrupt the other normal flow of work in the office? What effects does that have?"

Note: For the sake of brevity, several questions are grouped together above. In practice, of course, the sales person would ask one question, and wait for the answer before asking the next.

DM: "This kind of crunch happens frequently. To deal with the volume then, the typists and secretaries have to put in a lot of overtime. The firm also uses temporary typing services, as needed. Other typing gets delayed. Sometimes, if the need is especially pressing, we'll see $200-per-hour lawyers doing their own typing on their personal computers, just to get things out in time. That's very costly to us."

SP: "How do the secretaries and typists feel about this overtime?"

DM: "They get hefty pay for overtime, but they're usually not happy about having to work evenings and weekends. That gets old very quickly. As a result, a number of secretaries and typists have left the firm because they were not willing to spend that much time away from their families. In many cases, those we lost tended to be the best people, burned out by the constant overtime work-load."

SP: "We've been hearing a lot lately of secretarial burnout in other firms, as well, and they've had a great deal of trouble in replacing them because good legal secretaries and legal typists are so hard to find. Do you have any difficulties in replacing the people who have left?"

DM: "We sure do. Even when we are able to find experienced people, it usually still takes several months before they become fully productive."

Question testing value

SP: "That's expensive. Have you ever put a dollar figure on what it costs to replace a secretary or typist?"

DM: "We've never run the figures, but I'm sure that with all factors taken into account it costs several thousand dollars each time."

Another question to test value

SP: "You mentioned earlier that your firm used temporary typists to help out with crunch periods. Do you have any idea of what that costs in a typical year?"

DM: "As a matter of fact I do have a good handle on that, as our accountants break our costs out into categories. It was $13,000 last year."

Focusing-in questions

Here the sales person is recycling back to pick up on something said earlier, in order to establish another need or aspect of the need.

SP: "I'd like to backtrack a bit. Have you ever missed a filing deadline because you weren't able to get the volume of typing done in time?"

DM: "Knock on wood, we've never missed a deadline. But it has been close at times. More than once we've ended up chartering a plane to fly papers to other cities in order to meet filing deadlines."

Testing value

Though the following is a statement rather than a question, it serves the function of a question in drawing out the DM.

SP: "I expect it is very costly when you have to charter a plane to make a filing deadline."

DM: "Sometimes there's no alternative. It's either hire the plane, or lose the case by default and face a suit for malpractice. It's not a cost we can pass on to the client, since the delay was our problem. So we had to swallow the expense ourselves both times."

Focusing-in questions, again recycling to establish another area of need.

SP: "Going back to something you said earlier, you seem to have quite a high ratio of secretaries and typists to attorneys. Are they busy most of the time, or are many of them `bench strength' for when you need additional typing help?"

DM: "It's more bench strength than I'd like. I'd estimate that probably forty-percent of their time is spent waiting in reserve. It's hard to predict work-flow in this business. That's why we have to overstaff -- for reserve capacity when we need it. Yet there are still plenty of occasions when we don't have enough help when we need it."

SP: "Are you saying, then, that as much as forty-percent of your secretarial and typing staff is normally not needed? Is forty-percent of that cost wasted?"

DM: "Probably not the full forty-percent. But it is a fact that a large part of our payroll is wasted in this way."

SP: "Have you ever totaled what that comes to annually?"

DM: "I'm sure it comes to a great deal of money -- into six figures."

SP: "Let's do a quick check. As a ballpark figure, I'd estimate that your payroll for secretaries and typists totals around $5,000 per week, or $20,000 per month. Is that a reasonable estimate?"

DM: "That does sound reasonable."

SP: "Let's work that through. If we assume that just ten-percent of that represents wasted dollars because of overstaffing to be ready for crunch periods -- a conservative ten-percent, not the more likely forty-percent -- it still comes to $2,000 per month, or $24,000 per year."

DM: "That is a good bit of money. I hadn't looked at it that way before. And I agree that forty-percent is more likely, so that means we're wasting nearly $100,000 each year. I had no real awareness it amounted to that much!"

Summarizing

Here the SP summarizes and echoes back some of the key information that the DM has provided. From this, a pattern of needs emerges. This ties loose ends together into conclusions, and prepares the way for the next step, which is introducing the product, and showing how it meets these needs.

SP: "Clearly, getting critical typing done can be inordinately expensive in several ways. You mentioned, first of all, the consequences of overtime -- overtime pay, of course, but also the cost of losing your best people to burnout. You estimated that the cost of replacing and training came to several thousand dollars each. You mentioned that your accountant found that the firm spent $13,000 last year for temporary typists, mostly to help out with crunch periods. When the typing got behind and you were pressed to make filing deadlines, you twice needed to charter planes to deliver the documents -- at a cost of several thousand dollars each time. Additionally, by conservative estimate, at least $24,000 in secretarial and typist time are wasted in a typical year because of the need to overstaff to meet crunch periods. Had you realized before today just how much money this is costing the firm?"

DM: "Frankly, I had never put it all together. I've been too busy practicing law to look at it all in context. I'm stunned."

Testing value

In a transitional question, the SP attempts to get the DM to express overall interest. The question also opens the way for the next phase of the selling process, which is linking the benefits of the product to the DM's needs.

SP: "Suppose I could show you a way of getting all of this typing done on time at crunch periods, and still saving this $13,000 now spent on temporary typists. Would you be interested?"

DM: "We would be very interested."

If the prospect resists answering questions

If the Prospect says she feels your fact-finding questions will be a waste of time, or if she begins showing impatience part-way through, that's a sign that you haven't set the context clearly enough in explaining why you need this information.

In that case, say that you can't yet be sure precisely how you will be able to help her organization, but feel the chances justify the investment of a few more minutes. Your experience in similar businesses indicates that there will be a benefit from this effort.

Of course, there is another possible reason if the DM tires of your questions: from her perspective, the questions may not seem to be leading anywhere. You may need to better focus your questions, or you may need to break off from the questions and give an overview of what you are driving at.

PART FOUR: SHOWING HOW YOU CAN FILL THAT NEED

The central question addressed in Part Four is, How can I strengthen the value of my product in the Decision Maker's mind?

Recall the basic principle: organizations, and the Decision Makers within them, buy if and only if they arrive at solidly Yes answers to four questions:

1. Do we face a need?

2. Is that need significant enough to justify our spending some money to fill it?

3. Will this product or service actually fill that need?

4. Will it fill the need better or more cost-effectively than other approaches?

We examined the how-to behind the first two of these questions in Part Three. Now we'll be examining the impact of questions 3 and 4.

Chapter 14: Making The Links— From Prospect's Needs to Your Solution to the Value of Filling Those Needs

Once the Decision Maker is aware of the crucial needs (or needs), your next two steps follow:

To make the link clear between that need (or multiple needs), and precisely how your product or service will fill the need. (This is the subject of the present chapter.)

To deal in a positive way with the issues of cost and value. (The how-to of this is the subject of the next chapter.)

Presenting the selling logic visually

These two steps tie closely together, with one leading into the next. In your sales call, you will transition back and forth from Needs to Solutions to the Value of filling those needs. The selling logic goes like this:

NEEDS	SOLUTION	VALUE OF FILLING THE NEED
"We found these needs . . . "	"My product can fill these needs in these specific ways . . . "	"Even better: by using my product to fill those needs, it can pay for itself in these ways . . . "

That selling logic (NEED SOLUTION VALUE) provides the framework for a simple but effective visual aid.

You can prepare this selling visual aid on the spot with the DM as you take notes.

Or, you can use the framework as a model as you prepare more elaborate visual aids, such as overhead transparencies or flip-charts for a stand-up presentation.

You can also adapt the model to form a chart in a letter or written proposal.

NEEDS	PROPOSED SOLUTION	VALUE OF FILLING THE NEED

Chapter 15: Raising The Issues Of "Cost" And "Value:" Showing How Your Product Or Work More Than Pays For Itself.

Remember the selling logic, as in the previous chapter:

NEEDS	SOLUTION	VALUE OF FILLING THE NEED
"We found these needs . . . "	"My product can fill these needs in these specific ways . . . "	"Even better: by using my product to fill those needs, it can pay for itself in these ways . . . "

In previous chapters, we focused on ways of making the first linkage clear to the DM: that is the Need-to-Solution linkage.

Now we bring in the second key part of that linkage: showing how your product can -- either partly or totally -- pay for itself. This gets us into the issues of "price" (or "cost)," and "value." There is a major difference between the concepts of price (or cost) and value:

Price focuses on the dollars spent . . . while *value* puts price in the context of what is gained in exchange for those dollars.

Thus "talking value" to customers means showing how they will get back $1.01 or $1.25 or even $2.00 for each dollar they spend with you.

The prospect will naturally want to know the cost (or price) of your product or service, so you can't avoid providing that cost figure.

But if you are an effective sales person, you won't let things bog down on cost. Instead, quickly move on, shifting the Decision Maker's attention from cost alone to the broader issue of what she gets in return for that price paid.

That broader issue -- of what is gained in exchange for what we pay -- is the concept of Value.

Price is important in selling, of course, but is rarely the decisive factor in whether or not you make the sale. Generally, what really matters is value -- what the buyer gets in return for the money spent. (Another way of expressing that concept of value is its "cost-effectiveness.")

Effective Decision Makers will naturally be inclined to look beyond price to the really important issue of overall, long-term value.

But not all Decision Makers will start with that kind of vision, so a major part of your role as sales person is to "educate" this type of prospect to look with a different perspective.

The Four-Step Approach to building awareness of value
In "talking price" with the Decision Maker, the key is NEVER talk price ... EXCEPT in context.

That is, *don't let the prospect's focus remain on price alone*. Instead, guide the discussion so the DM views the money spent in the context of what is gained in exchange. In guiding that discussion, it's helpful to work through this Four-Step process.

1. Review the SPECIFIC NEEDS you uncovered.

Speak not just of needs in general, or of the typical needs of most customers, but rather the actual needs that turned up as you worked with this Decision Maker. Model:

- *"In the course of our meeting today, we found that you face two major needs. The first is _____ ."*

2. Review the SPECIFIC WAYS in which your product will fill each of those needs.

Your review of 1: Specific Needs, and 2: Specific Ways will usually be brief -- just enough to serve as a quick reminder to the DM of what you discussed earlier. Example:

- *"We found that the _____ feature of the GEM 2000 can resolve the first of these needs, by ___"*

3. Present PRICE.

There's no reason to be defensive or apologetic about what your product costs. If it's a good product that meets important needs of this organization, then naturally you deserve a fair price for it. If you are defensive on the matter of cost, the DM will sense this. But do not linger on price. Mention it, then move on to item 4.

4. Immediately TRANSITION FROM PRICE TO THE VALUE OF THE SOLUTION you offer.

Price and value naturally flow together, so the transition should flow easily. One way is to restate the price in a broader context. Sample:

- *"But let's look at that overall dollar cost in context. For example, you earlier told me that getting this work done using your present method takes 200 working hours each month. You estimated that these*

200 hours cost at least $3000 in direct labor, plus at least that much again in overhead -- that is, a total of $6000 each month.

- *"By contrast, you can have a GEM 2000 for $500 per month on lease. Add seven hours working time for that one operator at a cost of $100 per month, and the cost will total only $600 per month, instead of the present $6,000 per month. This means a saving of $5400 every month."*

- *"In other words, a GEM 2000 installation will cost only one-tenth as much as your present system. That's very good value for the money spent. Do you agree?"*

Chapter 16: Using Other Methods of Highlighting Value Over Cost

A quick review of where we are: helping the prospect move beyond the short-term cost of your product or service to view that price or cost in the context of the overall value gained.

Price, remember, focuses on dollars spent, Value puts cost in the context of what is gained. Thus, to make sales, show your prospects how they can get back $1.01 or more for each $1.00 spent.

The selling logic for helping the Decision Maker develop a sense of that Need > Solution > Value logic is expressed in this diagram:

NEEDS	SOLUTION	VALUE OF FILLING THE NEED
"We found these needs . . . "	"My product can fill these needs in these specific ways . . . "	"Even better: by using my product to fill those needs, it can pay for itself in these ways . . . "

In establishing this linkage, it's helpful to take the Prospect with you through a four-step process:

- Review the specific **needs** you uncovered.

- Review the specific ways in which your product will **fill each of those needs**.

- Present **price**.

- Immediately transition from price to the value of the solution you offer.

The core is simple, so don't let the words get in the way when you're with a prospect: when you present the price or cost of your product, put that cost into the context of the benefits the DM gets for that money spent.

That is, show the Value, and Value is showing how the DM gets back the equivalent of $1.01 or more for each $1.00 spent.

Alternative ways of expressing value
Basically, value is getting back $1.01 or more for each $1.00 spent.

But different customers may have different ideas of what they "value." One Decision Maker, for example, may operate with a long-term perspective, and may be looking for the benefits over a one-year span, while another may, by the nature of his job, be looking for a shorter-term value. Hence, to be successful you will need to adapt to the customer's perspective and mind-set.

But you need to be flexible in how you approach value. Some prospects will, literally, be looking for a dollars-and-cents kind of value (expressed in dollar terms), while others will be looking for their version of "value" not in dollars-and-cents terms, but in intangible forms such as convenience, status, quality, ease of use, assured service, or any of dozens of other forms.

Therefore, in presenting value, adapt your approach to the actual factors that specific DM "values" most. Precisely what she "values" will vary with the individual, with the situation, and with your product.

How to know what that individual values? As always in selling, the key is to listen well, both to what is said and implied. The DM may have already told you this, either overtly or implicitly. A Decision Maker, for instance, who speaks repeatedly about the costs and frustrations of a competing product is telling you that he strongly values reliability and good service.

Also, think back to your earlier fact-finding in the organization, before you first met with the DM: what themes and needs revealed themselves? For instance, if you see that the client organization's own sales literature focuses on economy and low cost, take that as a hint to make the case for the ways in which your product or service can lower their costs, or boost efficiency and productivity.

Ways of highlighting value over cost

The four-step process is the basic method for establishing value, but there are some other ways of highlighting value over cost that may be helpful within the four-step framework.

1. Break down the overall cost of your product into more meaningful units.

For example:

- *"The cost of the Model III is $4,000. That breaks down to about $16 per week over the normal five-year life of the unit. You'd agree, wouldn't you, that it's well worth about $3 per day for having this kind of convenience ready-at-hand?"*

- *Or, "That cost translates to about $5.00 per day in order to gain the advantages of superior quality and service."*

2. Restate the savings that will result into a form that is most attractive to this customer.

In putting cost in context, you can sometimes express the same cost saving in two or more alternative ways. For example, you could point out how installing the computer system you propose would "save the costs of one half-time employee." Alternately, you could suggest "it will free half of your secretary's time for other, more creative work."

Or, you could even restate it both ways, for double benefit: "You can use the time savings either to free your secretary for other more important assignments, or to reduce the use of overtime."

3. Refer to any incidental payoffs that add value.

Earlier, we suggested that you not throw a laundry-list of things your product can do at a customer. Instead, focus on only those benefits that match specific identified needs.

Well, now IS the time to refer to some of those additional "laundry-list" benefits, since these incidental payoffs, if raised at this point, may add enough extra value to nudge the customer to Yes.

If, for instance, you are selling phone equipment, you might find that of the equipment's dozen key benefits, only three or four specifically match the stated needs of this customer. Yet, once you have clearly established how the product will meet those three or four key needs, you may clinch the sale by raising a few more of those unmentioned capabilities as "bonuses."

Think of your own psychology when you're buying something. You finally find a product that precisely meets your needs. You're satisfied and are inclined to buy, but you're still on the fence, not sure you really want to spend the money.

While you're wavering, the sales person tells you that if you buy today you'll also get a free bonus (or frequent traveler coupon) thrown in at no extra cost. Very possibly, this something extra just might push you over the edge to buy now -- though it would have been only a distraction if the sales person had mentioned it earlier. While you wouldn't buy just to get the "freebie," the reality is that if you were wavering on whether to buy or not, it might be just enough to nudge you to Yes.

4. Use the analogy of the telephone.

But suppose the Decision Maker insists that low cost is the one factor that controls her purchasing decisions, and quality of product, ease of use, convenience and everything else are all but insignificant.

Respond by pointing out that if cost is of such paramount concern, then this organization could choose to operate with only a single telephone line, and only one phone receiver. The company could save hundreds of dollars each month if the staff shared that one phone for all of their incoming and outgoing business calls. Indeed, to save even more on the phone bill, the company could send all employees down to the pay phone on the corner.

But, of course, no firm chooses to do this, even though it would lower cash outlays for phone expenses. Instead, most companies wisely invest in extra lines and extra phones so there is one at every desk, because the value of the employees' time far outweighs the possible cost savings that might be gained from skimping on phones.

Moreover, image and convenience to customers are important factors to be considered: if customers couldn't get through on that pay phone they would go to another supplier, and the lost sales would quickly dwarf the phone bill.

After you have gotten this message across, transition to your specific product, showing how -- like phone service -- its costs are minimal in comparison with the benefits it brings.

What if the prospect insists on forcing the issue to price alone?

Repeating the overall point made in this chapter: most of the time it is best to try to move the customer's focus from a narrow emphasis on price alone to a broader perspective that encompasses the more important matter of cost-effectiveness. ("Cost-effectiveness," remember, can be thought of as another name for "value.")

However, there will be times when you have no choice other than to talk price, because "price" seems to be the only word in the customer's vocabulary. Even in those cases, though, you can treat price in a positive rather than defensive way.

Case 1. Show how your product offers more value (more cost-effectiveness) than does the competing product.

What if your price is significantly higher than the competition's? In that case, you will probably lose unless you can "educate" the customer on the unique benefits of your offering. To do this, shift the discussion back to value, as we have discussed above.

Case 2. Contrast the price against the cost of NOT FILLING THE NEED.

In this situation, the customer is saying, "We can't afford it," to which your reply is "You can't afford to be without it." That is, put price in context with what hidden costs would result from not having it.

Summary

Price is important, but rarely is as decisive as you might expect.

More important than price is Value. While Price focuses on dollars spent, Value puts cost in the context of what is gained.

To make sales, show your prospects how they can get back $1.01 or more for each $1.00 spent.

To build the DM's awareness of Value, speak of price only in context, never by itself. Generally, that means working through a four-step process:

1. Review the specific needs you uncovered.

2. Review the specific ways in which your product will fill each of those needs.

3. Present price.

4. Immediately transition from price to the value of the solution you offer.

Other methods of highlighting value over cost:

1. Restate costs in more meaningful units.

2. Restate cost in an alternative way that is more meaningful to this customer.

3. Refer to any "incidental payoffs" that add value.

4. Use the analogy of the telephone.

However, there will be times when the customer is determined to look not at overall value but rather at short-term cost. Even then, treat price in a positive rather than defensive way, such as,

1. Show how your product offers more value (that is, more cost-effectiveness) than does any competing product or approach.

2. Speak of price, but then transition to a comparison of price versus the cost of not having what you propose.

Chapter 17: Making Your Sales Points Clearly and Concisely

In making clear the linkage between the customer's Needs, the Solution you propose, and the Value it offers, you can use any of a variety of methods. You can:

1. Use a chart or visual aid to make the need-to-features linkage clear.

A simple chart (like the one we've been using here) can provide helpful structure to that communication, giving the DM a mental framework upon which to see the specific need-to-feature linkages.

NEEDS	PROPOSED SOLUTION	VALUE OF FILLING THE NEED

But don't just put a chart in front of the Prospect and take for granted that it makes as much sense to her as to you. It's important that the links between the Prospect's needs and your product, as well as the value the product gives, are totally clear and explicit in the Prospect's mind.

Therefore, don't let the chart stand alone. Instead, use it as a visual aid in talking the Prospect through precisely how you product fills the specific needs of this specific buyer.

Whenever possible, echo the words the prospect used in telling you of the need:

- *"You mentioned earlier that your department was having difficulties in ... Well, the GEM 2000 can help you overcome that difficulty by ..."*

Sometimes you will need not only to explain how your product fills the customer's needs, but also to prove it. We examine proof sources later in this book.

2. Demonstrate your product or samples.

In some cases, it's practical to make the link between need and solution clear simply by showing your product (or the results of the service you perform).

For example, if you're marketing your services as a graphic designer, you might demonstrate your ability to fill this customer's needs by showing some relevant samples of the work you've done for other clients.

Similarly, if you are marketing consulting services, this might be the point to reach into your briefcase and pull out appropriate samples from other projects you've handled.

In an earlier chapter, I discouraged using samples of your product or work to "speak for itself" in creating its own need in the customer's mind. If you expect the product or samples to create the need, you'll usually be disappointed.

Here I'm suggesting a different way of using your work samples. That is by using these not in hopes of creating the DM's sense of need, but rather to prove that your product can do what you claim it can.

Once the need is clear to the DM, then he'll be interested in determining whether your product can fill that need. It's at that point that samples -- or perhaps the item itself -- become relevant, as they can often make that clear in a way that words, or even pictures, cannot.

3. Use your sales literature as a tool to make the linkage clear.

Earlier, I suggested that you not hand your brochures or other promotional literature to the DM at the start of the sales call, as he would be distracted by these printed materials, and might not be listening with full attention to your sales presentation.

But now, as you make the link between the customer's need and the capabilities of your product, may be a good time to use that literature. However, you can't just hand a brochure over the desk and expect it to make the point.

At the very least, talk the DM through the relevant parts of your literature, pointing out how your features and capabilities mesh with his needs. But make those capabilities explicit: Don't take for granted that the DM will get the point you're making.

- *"We concluded that you needed _____ . Well, as you see in this illustration, the GEM 2000 has a (fill in the capability), which can achieve the (fill in the need), which you need."*

Getting on the same side of the table

An even better way to use your sales literature: Use the brochure as a tool for positioning yourself and the Decision Maker literally "on the same side of the table." Here's what I mean, and how to do it:

A manager's desk is a status symbol, and a barrier between that DM and the rest of the world. The desk or conference table "sets up a wall," marking off "us" (this side of the desk) from "them" (those across the desk).

If you can break down or get around that barrier, somehow getting yourself over to the DM's side of the desk or conference table, then you can literally "get on the same side," and "get your heads together," in working jointly to solve the problem.

Your brochure can serve as a ticket around to the DM's side of the desk. When the brochure becomes relevant (as now, when you're making the link), say,

- *"There's something I'd like us to look at together. May I bring my chair around?"*

Provided there's a reasonable amount of space, the DM can hardly object. Once you get on the DM's side of the desk, you'll usually find that, quite literally, the psychological barrier eases, if not dissolves altogether.

We'll address non-verbal communication, positioning yourself and the customer, and related subtleties, in a later chapter: Sending and Receiving Non-Verbal Messages

Marking up your sales literature to make key points

Mark up the brochure as you review it with the DM. Customize it to highlight the special interests of this prospect by circling or highlighting the key points that are relevant to this prospective client. Draw special diagrams, underline, add highlights, do whatever you need to make it clear just how your product fits the DM's needs.

After all, it's just a give-away, so there's no reason at all why it should stay pristine, and if your marks help the DM remember your key selling messages, then don't hesitate.

Focus on what your product (or service) does, not what it is

One more time: What the customer is ultimately interested in is NOT what your product IS, but rather what it DOES to fill his or her specific need.

For example, the Decision Maker's interest will generally not be in technology for its own sake, but rather in the practical results -- particularly as these results improve the workings of his or her area of responsibility. It's the same with non-business clients: their interest is in what your product will do for them, not for what it is.

Your product may do many things, but in demonstrating it to your prospect, focus only on those aspects that directly relate to that customer's specific needs -- that is, the needs which have been clearly identified in your earlier conversation. Do not clutter your message with incidental benefits that are not directly relevant for this Decision Maker and this organization.

People and organizations buy to meet specific, identified needs -- that is, they buy to solve identified problems, not to stockpile generic capabilities. A generalized approach that treats all features equally will inevitably miss the important targets -- this specific DM's specific needs.

It's not enough simply to throw out some of the things your product can do and hope they stick with the prospect. Nor is it enough to demonstrate the product, or to give the Decision Maker samples, and expect the link between the DM's needs and the capabilities of your product to be obvious.

Your "Half-Minute Messages"

You will quickly develop a sense of the most common kinds of customer needs, and of how the various features or aspects of your product (or service) can fill those needs.

Though each customer's needs may be somewhat unique, they will fall into patterns. Therefore invest the time to boil down into short, to-the-point messages the way in which specific features or aspects of your product match those common need areas.

Polish these messages. Edit out extraneous words, and simplify the sentences so you can say them comfortably in not more than 30 seconds, in your normal conversational style. (Tip: short sentences make points clearly, and are easy to speak in a way that sounds natural and spontaneous.)

Rehearse these Half-Minute Selling Messages until they flow smoothly and confidently. Take care so they don't sound rehearsed or "canned." Even though you may have said it hundreds of times, it's all new to this customer, and should sound fresh.

As a rule of thumb, each statement (or "selling message") should take you less than a half-minute -- at most -- to say. If you talk more than that on a topic, the customer's eyes -- and mind -- will likely glaze over.

Besides, if you go on for more than about 30 seconds on any single point, you'll tend to begin "talking at" the Decision Maker, rather than carrying on a productive back-and-forth dialogue.

"Netting-it-out"

In making the link between your product and the customer's needs . . . Get to the point. "Net out" your messages. Keep in mind that the object is to make the sale, not to say everything possible about the product.

In speaking of your product and how it fills the customer's needs, be focused. Get to the point. Make your point, once, then move on. Don't overwhelm with words. Respect the DM's valuable time. Trust the DM: if she needs to know more, or if you failed to make a point clearly, she'll let you know -- either verbally or non-verbally.

Summary

Customers buy to fill needs. Before they will buy, though, they must be consciously aware of the needs, and the needs must seem significant enough to be worth the time, effort, and budget it will cost to take action.

If the customer is to buy your product, it must be totally clear to the customer that your product will in fact fill those needs. Don't assume that what is obvious to you is equally clear to the customer.

In introducing your product or service, focus on the practical results for the user. Customers, after all, will buy not for what your product IS, but rather for what it DOES.

As you present your product, emphasize those capabilities that fill the specific needs of this customer. Don't talk about how wonderful your product is in general. Instead, show how its specific capabilities will fill the customer's specific needs.

Thus, relate each capability of your product back to one of the specific needs which you identified earlier in your discussion with the decision maker. If possible, echo back her own words as she described the need and what that unfilled need was costing.

Finally, get to the point. "Net out" your messages. Keep in mind that the object is to make the sale, not to say everything you possibly could about the product.

Three main ways are available for you to make a clear, visual linkage between the customer's needs and the capabilities of your product or service to fill that need:

1. Use a chart or visual aid to make the need-to-features linkage clear.

2. Demonstrate your product or samples as a way of proving that the product can do what you claim.

3. Use your sales literature as a tool to make that linkage clear.

PART FIVE: CONVINCING THE DECISION MAKER TO ACT NOW!

The core question addressed in this Part: How can I get the Decision Maker to move on this NOW, and not just "think about it?"

By this point in the sales cycle, you've helped the Decision Maker perceive that there is a significant need, and that your product or service can fill that need in a cost-effective way.

Now you need to nudge that DM to take some "buying action." Precisely what type of "buying action" you seek will depend upon the situation.

In this Part, we examine about a dozen ways of asking the Decision Maker to take buying action. It's helpful to be able to call upon a repertoire of varied approaches so you can ask and ask again without coming across as "pushy."

In addition to the actual methods of asking the DM to buy, we also look at some related issues in this Part:

How do you recognize when the DM is ready to take some buying action? That is, what "buying signals" indicate that now is the time to attempt to "close" the sale? (We look at this is Chapter 18.)

Also, when you ask the DM to take "buying action," just what kind of actions can you reasonably ask for? Most of the time, the action will be the obvious one of buying your product or service. But in some cases, that may be too large a step to ask for initially, so you may instead ask the DM to take or authorize some intermediate step that must be completed before you can actually conclude the sale.

For example, you might ask the DM to attend a demonstration of your product in action, or you might ask for a commitment that if you are able to prove your case through a financial proposal, they will buy.

On hearing no

For people new to selling, asking the DM to buy or take other action may be a little scary. No one likes to hear No. But keep in mind that the worst thing is not hearing No; the worst thing is failing to get the sale you could have had.

Scary as it may be when you're new to selling, taking that risk of asking for the order is essential. By asking for action, you signal that you have made your basic case, and now the next move is up to the DM.

Until you ask the DM to act, nothing -- absolutely nothing at all -- is likely to happen. If you want something good to happen -- that is, for the sale to happen -- then you have to ask for it to happen.

Why no can be good news

When you ask, Yes is the ideal answer.

But even No is a positive step, as it gives an opening to probe further, in order to find out what is really bothering the DM. Once you hear No, you can get down to the real business of helping the DM change his mind.

But if you must hear No, then the sooner the better. Once you get the DM to move off the "undecided" square and say either Yes or No, then the way is opened for you to take the next step. You can either write the order, or openly probe what specific obstacles are blocking this sale. Once that No is out in the open, you can be more direct in finding what's really keeping the DM from buying. No opens the way to move to Yes.

Even in the worst case -- when the No just can't be overturned -- hearing that No early at least lets you cut your losses sooner, and move on to find more promising prospects.

Why it pays to complete the order blank before you go into the sales call

Many of the best sales people with whom I have worked make a practice of filling in the sales order form before going into the meeting with the DM. It takes a little time, and some order blanks will get thrown away. But the benefits make it worth the while.

For one thing, you don't have to stop the sales momentum in the call to collect basic data on things such as address, billing address and the like. Even more importantly, by completing the form in advance you project to the DM your confidence that the sale will, naturally, happen. Expectations are infectious, and a large part of selling is projecting positive expectations.

Pre-call planning: determining what to close for

In the jargon of professional sales people, asking for the order or other commitment is "closing." You might "close" the customer, or "close for" the order. You might try several different "closes."

Before going into any sales call, think through your primary and backup objectives for that call. The range of objectives includes:

Closing for the Order.

In the ideal case, your primary objective will be to close for the sale. That's the ideal, but in some cases it may not be realistic. For example, it's not likely that you will meet with a DM for the first time, and walk out of that meeting with a $50,000 order. It could happen, but it's not likely. On the other hand, if yours is a low-cost item, you can't afford to make many call-backs.

Closing for the DM's agreement to continue the sales cycle with you.

With some products (and in some price ranges), the typical selling cycle might extend over two or three or a half-dozen calls. The first call might be to introduce yourself and your product, and to make the first cut at assessing needs. Later calls may be for the purpose of conducting more detailed needs analysis, and other fact-gathering. In still later calls in the cycle, you may introduce "proof sources," such as demonstrations or cost proposals.

In longer sales cycles, you should "close" the DM before proceeding to the next step. It isn't enough for the DM to passively assent to your coming back another time. Instead, you would the DM's clearly-expressed commitment that he is interested enough to have you proceed. There is no point in your investing time and effort if the DM is only going through the motions if the DM is only going through the motions with you.

Closing for at least the chance to come back and try again another time.

This is the basic fallback position: if you can't get the DM to say Yes now, then at least try to keep the door open so he agrees that it would be a good idea for you to call back perhaps in a few months, or when conditions have changed, or when your product has been updated to better meet his needs..

It's important to plan in advance what your sequence of objectives will be with this customer, because selling is a fast-breaking game. Things happen that you can't anticipate, and you don't want to find yourself boxed into a corner -- or find yourself walking out of the door without no order in hand, and no graceful way to come back later.

By having your sequence of alternate objectives in mind, you can back-off from pushing for an action that the customer clearly will not take today. If you see the way to a sale is closed, you can transition to an alternative that makes sense with this particular customer. For example, you could shift from going for the sale to inviting the customer to agree to a demonstration or a free or low-cost trial

Chapter 18: Recognizing Buying Signals

Back in Chapter 4, we took a look at some of the buying signals you might encounter from the Decision Maker's Screen as you try to set up an initial appointment. These signals, mostly over the phone, included,

- Change in manner or tone;

- Questions that indicated interest;

- Statements that implied that they were won over, so the only real points at issue were the details such as time and place.

But it's not only Screens who give you useful buying signals: an interested Decision Maker will bristle with positive signs that are there to be read. It's important to remain alert to these signals, as they can tell you -- even before the Screen or Decision Maker may know it himself -- that he is ready to buy, or nearly ready.

Indeed, there will be times when the Decision Maker's buying signals are so strong and positive that there is no break between your presentation and the DM's agreement: it's as if there is one continuous flow to the communication. In those happy cases, you don't really need to ask for the order, as the DM's words or actions make it clear that all that remains is to work out the details.

The actual buying signal" will depend to a large extent on the individual's unique mannerisms, so you'll need to be alert and flexible. To get started, attune to basic areas such as those following.

Non-Verbal Signals.

If the DM is sitting forward on his chair, nodding his head, muttering words like, "Great! Exactly what we need! Yes, I see how it fits in," then you have strongly positive buying signals. That is probably the point at which you should stop trying to persuade the DM, and instead move on to wrap it up by closing for some kind of buying action.

Questions and comments.

It's usually a positive signal when the DM begins asking about practical matters, such as, "How soon can you deliver? or "Is it available in (a certain color or size or other similar detail)?" Questions of this sort imply that the DM has basically made the decision to buy, and now has moved on to settle the details.

Certain kinds of objections can be buying signals.

If a DM asks detailed questions about your product, or about how it differs from your competition, you probably have a signal of interest. After all, busy people don't get into the details unless they see a good reason for them to do so. The fact that the DM is interested enough to explore this kind of practical issue signals that the DM is at least testing the What-if of buying. The trend is positive, so be ready to move with that trend.

Interest in haggling over details.

The sale is probably yours if the DM initiates tentative negotiating probes over matters that would be relevant only if the sale is going through. (In other words, this indicates that you have *almost* made the sale . . . provided you can negotiate mutually-agreeable terms.)

For instance, a DM might say, "You're talking about too long a lead time before you can install. The delay is costing me money." But analyze what she is saying beneath the words, which probably is, "I'm ready to buy, provided you can speed up delivery."

Incidentally, these buying signals by the DM may not be consciously sent, so it's important to look through the actual words and gestures to find what is really meant or implied. In this case, the DM may not have actually decided to buy -- at least not on a conscious level -- but the interest in delivery times betrays what's really going on in his mind. If you're attuned to that, you can adapt as appropriate.

Chapter 19: Asking the Decision Maker to Take Buying Action

There's no single best way of asking for the order, or other "buying commitment." In this Chapter, we examine three of the most widely useful approaches, then another eight more methods in the next.

However, before we get into specific ways of asking for the order, it is helpful to focus on two overall strategies that will be useful regardless of how you ask for the order.

Two basic strategies in asking for action

Later in this chapter, we'll be focusing on specific ways of asking the DM to take buying action. Before we do that, though, we need to examine a pair of strategies that are useful as you ask the DM to take action.

First: Project the assumption that the Prospect will *naturally* agree.

That's a reasonable assumption. After all, you've invested your time and best efforts in working with the DM to diagnose real needs. Then, drawing on your experience and expertise, you've proposed a sound, cost-effective way of filling those needs. Viewed in that context, it makes perfect sense that the DM will naturally choose to implement your recommendations.

But your confidence and enthusiasm must be contagious. Some suggestions on communicating that assumption:

Project enthusiasm by energetic body language.

Sit forward in the chair as people do when they are interested and excited. Talk a little faster and a little louder than normal (unless, of course, you're already notorious for talking too loud and fast).

Project confidence and positive expectations verbally.

Avoid tentative expressions that communicate uncertainty. Instead, speak as though the other person has decided in your favor. Say things like, "When you install our system, not "If you install it."

Speak clearly and with energy in your voice.

Project the sense that you are enthusiastic about your product or service, and that it is still exciting and new to you ... and, hence, that the DM should also find it just as exciting. Don't make the mistake of quickly mumbling through your sales message, or of reciting it mechanically. You may be saying things you have said a hundred times before, but don't let that show: it's all new to the DM.

Communicate by the level of the investment your effort.

Subtle things can make significant impressions. For example, by taking the time to fill out the order blank before you arrive at the DM's office, you subtly signal your confidence that the decision will naturally be in your favor. One way of communicating your investment of effort is to complete a detailed Action Plan for installing your product. In this Action Plan, use actual calendar dates such as "August 7," rather than the generic formats like "Two weeks after ordering."

The Prospect will be impressed that you bothered to think through the plan specifically for this organization. He may infer that since you invested this level of effort, not only were you confident that the product is right for the firm, but that you can be counted on to be organized, professional, and on-time.

Second: After asking for action, be silent. Wait for a response. Once you ask, leave it up to the DM to respond . . . no matter how long the silence lasts.

Once you ask for the order, stop talking. By asking for action, you put the ball in the DM's court. You have asked a question; now let the silence hang heavy while the DM decides how to respond.

Your silence gives the DM time to think. It also adds pressure, because most people find silence uncomfortable. Don't rush in to rescue the DM from this pressure. After all, it is the Decision Maker's own delay now that is causing this uncomfortable silence. The DM himself has the power to ease that pressure by responding to your question.

The silence and resulting pressure will usually be on your side, as it forces the DM to make a decision to end that silence. If your presentation has made sense, then the DM will be pushed to say Yes. With the silence hanging, he may find it hard to come up with any good reason to say No.

But even if he does say No, then you can probe to find the reasons. Again, as you ask these probing questions, use the power of silence. Ask a question, then wait for the answer . . . no matter how long it takes. If you butt in with another question to fill the silence, then you rescue the DM from making the decision.

Often, too, the pressure of the silence will cause the DM to blurt out the real reasons behind his hesitation. These underlying reasons may be quite different from what he has said earlier. For some people, "No" is just a habit they follow without really thinking. Your silence can break through that habit and force them to focus on the reality of the actual situation.

Basic closing approaches

1. Simple Direct Request for the Order.

Sometimes the positive signals will be so strong that little needs to be said, and the sale seems to wrap itself up. The simplest close follows this outline:

Summarize the key points made, highlighting the needs raised, and the ways in which your product will fill those needs.

Check for completeness. Make sure you have touched upon all matters of importance to the DM by asking something on the order of, "Is there anything else we need to talk about now?" If the DM does raise issues, deal with them, then summarize once again, and check for completeness again: "Can you think of anything else we should talk about?"

Then proceed to ask for the order.

2. Summary and Recommendations.

Briefly summarize both the key needs and the corresponding ways in which your product will fill these needs. Then test for completeness by asking a version of the question, "Is there anything that keeps us from proceeding with this?" (Or simply, "Anything else?")

Deal with any additional issues that come up, then ask for the action you need. Here's a model:

- *"To sum up, Ms. Barker, we discussed your need to increase productivity in the billing department, and at the same time to cut the expense of hiring temporary clerical workers. The GEM 4000 meets both of these needs. It will increase productivity by at least 20%, which will significantly reduce the need for temporary help by an estimated 15%. If you approve the plan now, we can have the GEM 4000 in place by the end of the week. Will that be soon enough, or shall I request a priority installation?"*

3. Action Plan (or "Implementation Schedule").

Here you again summarize the needs and the corresponding ways in which your product will fill those needs. Then show how you intend to put your proposals into operation, using a written action plan as a visual aid. Advantages of using an Action Plan (or Implementation Plan) as a tool for closing include,

You project your confidence that the purchase makes perfect sense. The DM will be impressed by the interest you show in going to the trouble of planning this implementation schedule even before the sale is locked in.

It is direct, to-the-point, and businesslike. The DM will respect your professionalism. The schedule shows that you know what you are doing, and that you plan ahead to make sure it will work as promised.

It will cause any final or hidden objections to surface now, so you can deal with them. After all, acceptance of the Action Plan implies assent to the purchase, so it becomes a matter of clarifying the hesitations, or living with them.

To use this approach, type out in advance a schedule, using a format similar to the example below, though adapt it to your specific needs.

Always use actual calendar dates like "April 1," instead of "10 days after signing." Even though you may later change these dates to reflect later discussions with the DM, they project your sense of confidence that the order will come through as the natural and inevitable outcome of your sales efforts.

The "Who is Responsible" column shows that you have thought it through. It clarifies both what you do, and what cooperation you will need from the DM's organization. If necessary, include here mention of what actions or other support are needed from the DM's organization, such as approvals, preliminary funding, or other preparation like making space or working area available. (In the model below, "SELL Co." is the seller, and "BUY Inc." is the potential buyer.)

TASK	WHO IS RESPONSIBLE	DATE

Experiment with adapting this model to your product. What realistic tasks would be involved, with what time frames? What actions would you need to take in order to install, and what cooperation would you need from the customer?

Summary

In asking the Prospect to take any kind of buying action, work with these two strategies in mind:

Project the assumption that the Decision Maker will naturally agree.

After you ask for action, be silent. Wait for a response. Let the Decision Maker respond . . . no matter how long it takes.

In projecting your confidence that the DM will naturally agree, be attuned to subtle aspects such as,

- Your body language: let your enthusiasm show.

- Your verbal language: for instance, say "When you buy," not "If you buy."

- The level of your effort invested: take the extra effort to project your confidence that you will get the order. For instance, come in with the customer's name and address already filled in on the order blank.

- Be attuned also to the customer's buying signals. Begin by looking for signals in these areas, but be open to other kinds of signals you'll encounter:

- The DM's body language and other non-verbal communications as they evidence enthusiasm and interest.

- The DM's questions and comments, if they imply readiness to proceed.

- The DM's interest in discussing or negotiating details that imply the sale may be taken for granted, consciously or sub-consciously.

There is no single best way of asking the customer to buy or take other action. But have a repertoire of different approaches ready, so you can ask again -- and again -- without sounding like a broken record. Here are three to get you started, with others explored in the chapter that follows.

1. Simple Direct Request.

2. Summary and Recommendations.

3. Action Plan.

SELLING 101   Michael McGaulley

Chapter 20: More Ways of Asking the Decision Maker to Take Action

When asking the Prospect to take any kind of buying action (whether to sign the order or to agree to some other step forward), work with two basic strategies in mind:

First: Project the assumption that the Decision Maker will naturally agree.

Second: After you ask for action, be silent. Wait for a response. Let the Decision Maker respond . . . no matter how long it takes.

In the previous chapter, we also addressed the how-to of three key ways of "closing" the sale and asking the DM to take buying action. These were,

1. Simple Direct Request.

2. Summary and Recommendations.

3. Action Plan.

In this Chapter, we carry on this process and examine eight additional ways of asking for the sale. You don't need to master them all before your first day of selling. Just get started, and know they're here for you when you've mastered the basics and are ready to expand your repertoire of methods.

One study among Xerox sales reps found that, on average, *it took six attempts* by the Sales Rep to close the sale before the Decision Maker typically agreed to buy. The point is, don't give up if you hear No, or even if you hear No again and again. Keep asking. As one put it, "Each time you hear No means you're that much closer to hearing the ultimate Yes."

4. The Similar Situation Technique.

Here the similar situation references how another organization acted when faced with a situation like that now facing the DM. You can take a negative tack and describe the difficulties that resulted because the other people did not buy your product.

Or, usually better, you can take a positive approach and describe the advantages they gained because they did buy from you. The positive approach allows the prospect to identify with success.

The similar situation closing approach works best if you can add credibility by citing actual names of organizations and decision makers. It also provides a concrete proof source.

Details on specific points of similarity are useful, as they enable the present prospect to identify more strongly with each benefit. But don't get bogged down on details: a sentence on each should be enough as a start. If the DM is seriously interested in your product and wants to know more, you can count on letting you know.

- *"A small accounting firm like yours installed our software last fall. By their own analysis, it had paid for itself by the end of the first week. The senior partner told me that her only regret was that they hadn't found it a year sooner. We can have it in operation for you 14 days from today. Will that been soon enough, or should I request special installation?"*

Incidentally, it's even better if you can name that other client, but be sure to get their clearance before doing so.

5. Last Chance.

Few things put the sense of urgency into a customer like a bargain that is about to slip away. "The sale ends today," or "This is the last one in stock at the old price," or "Our prices will be rising five percent effective the first of the month" all are powerful motivators to take action NOW.

6. Alternate Choice.

Here you present the DM with two and only two alternatives, phrased so that by choosing either alternative the DM is by implication saying yes to the basic proposal.

This approach is particularly useful with a DM who may be indecisive by nature, or who seems overwhelmed by the variety of possibilities from which to choose. By narrowing the range, you help him sharpen the focus.

In selecting which pair of alternatives to use, decide whether to focus the customer's choice on central or secondary issues.

Central issues. The alternatives on which you focus go to the heart of the matter: "Do you think Option A or Option B will be best for you?"

Secondary issues. Here you focus the decision on a choice between two less important issues, both of which imply assent to the sale you are proposing. You may have encountered a variation of this the last time you bought a new car, when the salesperson asked whether you "preferred" Misty Green or Azure Blue.

Granted, the Alternate Choice close can seem manipulative or "high-pressure," so if you're not comfortable with it, better not use it.

But, on the other hand, if you do try it, you'll be surprised at how easily it accomplishes the purpose without antagonizing customers. Many will respect your self-confidence in assuming that the sale makes such good sense. Others will appreciate your focusing the issues for them, so they can select more efficiently between alternatives.

7. The order-blank request

For this to work well, you need to plan for it from the start of the call. As soon as you sit with the Prospect, take out a fresh order-blank and put it in plain view. As you collect information on the customer's needs, print it on the form. (Remember: *before* going in to the DM's office, fill in the basic customer data such as the firm's name and address.)

At the end of your selling message, you do not ask the DM to buy. Instead, ask a question that implies that the sale has been agreed-to, such as "Will I need a purchase order?" or "Will you want it shipped here to 2210 Waverly?"

Similarly, when the order blank is complete, don't ask the DM to "sign" it. Instead, ask him to "authorize" or "okay" it.

8. The "Sharp-Angle" Request.

Suppose the DM asks a question about your product, such as whether it can be in place by the end of the month, or whether it can be obtained in a color to coordinate with the other office equipment.

Instead of immediately saying "Yes, of course," respond with another question that puts a condition on your yes. To do this, you might respond, "So you'd want it, provided it's available in that shade of blue?"

By making your reply seem conditional, your response becomes more valuable to the customer. Then your response becomes not just "Yes," but "Yes, I'll meet your request, provided you can reassure me that you are serious enough about this issue to be willing to buy if I supply what you are asking for."

Once the DM has assured you that he would indeed want it in blue (or whatever), then you can explain that you can indeed supply it as requested. Then immediately transition to the details of delivery, payment or the like, WITHOUT pausing to ask whether he does want to buy. (After all, you can rightly assume that he does in fact want it, given that he was interested enough to ask.)

An incidental benefit: the conditional question is also useful in sorting out those who are serious prospects from those who are only chatting with you to fill up the time until they can retire.

This works, naturally enough, only if you can say Yes to the DM's inquiry. If you know you can't supply it, do not say No. Instead, probe to find why that is important to the DM. If may turn out to be unimportant, and you can move on from it. If it is important, your probing may open up alternatives that can supply what the customer is ultimately after. (For example, you might find that he doesn't care so much about getting the product in blue, as in having a change from the color now in place.)

9. The Balance Sheet.

This is especially helpful when you're working with an indecisive prospect, or one whose responses are so vague that you can't quite focus on any specific objection to get your teeth into.

Take out a sheet of paper, and draw a line down the middle. On the top of one column, print "Reasons favoring." Print "reasons opposing" at the top of the second column.

REASONS FAVORING	REASONS OPPOSING

Then state the issue in a form like this: "It seems to me that the question you're facing is whether to go with the GEM 4000. Do you agree?"

Once the question has been defined in that way, focus on the reasons favoring the purchase. The prospect will already be able to list some of those reasons. Jot them in the appropriate column. Suggest any other favoring reasons that she overlooked.

When the positive list is complete, move on to work with the DM in coming up with the reasons opposing. Since they are her reasons for not wanting to buy, you shouldn't feel any need to provide additional help here.

When you're finished, the list of Reasons Favoring will probably be much longer than the Reasons Opposing. Point out that difference in the length of the lists, and ask for the order by saying, "The right choice seems obvious, doesn't it?"

What if the DM still hesitates? At least now you have a clear statement of what reasons are holding her back, because she has listed them for you in the Reasons Opposing column. Go over these one-by-one, eliminating each, using the Four-Step process for handling objections which you'll meet in Part Six.

Salvage tools

This last group of "closing methods" are primarily useful in salvaging the situation when nothing else seems to work, and you feel the sale is slipping away.

10. The "Final" Objection.

This is based on the Four-Step process for responding to objections that we cover in Part Six. You'll find the how-to at the end of Chapter 24 in that Part.

11. The Lost Sale (Also known as the "Columbo.")

The approach gets its name from the old TV series with Detective Columbo of the shaggy raincoat. Columbo interrogates a suspect, but gets nowhere. Columbo pulls himself to his feet, shuffles to the door, defeated. The suspect relaxes, thinking that it's over, the pressure is off. Then, half-way out the door, Columbo pokes his head back in with one final question, which happens to be the question that's at the core of it all. The suspect, caught off-guard, makes a fatal admission.

Use this when everything else has failed: the customer has given a final, definite No, and the sale seems lost. Pack up your briefcase, stand, start to leave. But just before going out the door, pause and say, as if it's an afterthought -- "I feel I should apologize."

The DM, will probably be surprised, and ask why you feel that way. Respond, "Because somehow or somewhere I've obviously failed to make the benefits clear to you. I'm certain that if I'd done a better job you'd see the value, and there'd be no doubt in your mind. I wonder, would you mind telling me where I went wrong? What could I have done better? Did I leave some questions unanswered?"

The DM may say "Get on out of here," but more often will be pleased to give you some advice.

But listen attentively, and look through the words to what is really being said. For instance, if the DM says it was simply a matter of lack of funds, it may be that you failed to explain alternative financing plans, or that you lacked a low-cost introductory offer.

Or, if the DM says the company prefers to buy from well-established firms, the real problem is that you failed to establish your credentials clearly enough. As a consequence, the prospect failed to look past the lack of a known name-tag to recognize the quality of your product, or the commitment of your company to stay in the marketplace.

Again, listen well, as this is valuable feedback. Learn from it before you make sales calls on other customers. But if you're really deft, you may also be able to use this feedback in one final attempt to salvage this "lost" sale: "I appreciate your giving me this feedback. I can see that, as you say, the cost factors were the key sticking point. And I apologize: I let you down. I neglected to make clear that we offer an extended payment plan that would let you install our product for an initial payment of only $_____ ."

Well, now you are Columbo the Sales Person, and you're just trying to help the customer. Can you help it if something the DM says triggers another line of thought?

Summary

Nothing -- absolutely nothing at all -- is likely to happen until you actually take the step of asking for the order (or "closing" for the order, to use sales-rep's jargon.) When you ask, you risk hearing No. But it's best to hear that No early, while you can still turn things around.

In asking for the order (or other buying commitment) follow these two basic principles:

First: As you ask, project the assumption that the Decision Maker will NATURALLY say Yes, since your proposal makes such perfect sense.

Second: After asking, BE SILENT. Wait for the Decision Maker's response before you say another word ... no matter how long that takes.

Among the most effective ways of asking for the DM's buying commitment are these:

Covered in the previous chapter:

1. Simple Direct Request.

2. Summary and Recommendations.

3. Action Plan.

Covered in this chapter:

4. Similar Situation.

5. Last Chance.

6. Alternate Choice.

7. Order-Blank Request.

8. Sharp-Angle Request.

9. Balance Sheet.

10. "Final" Objection. (For how-to, see Chapter 24.)

11. Lost Sale, or "Columbo."

PART SIX: COPING WITH QUESTIONS, OBJECTIONS, AND HESITATIONS

The core question addressed in this Part: What's the best way in this situation of responding to the Decision Maker's questions and objections, so the sale doesn't become blocked?

It's a fact of selling life that most of the time you'll hear either No or a strong reason not to buy the first time (and maybe even the second and third) time you ask for the order. (Recall the Xerox study I mentioned earlier that found that the typical sale came through only on the Sales Rep's sixth attempt to close.)

But it's also a fact that much -- if not most -- of the time, the tough objections you encounter, or even the flat "No," are intended only as trial balloons.

Consciously or sub-consciously, the Decision Maker may be thinking, "The easiest thing is to say No. No preserves the status quo; there's less risk that way. Besides, if this sales person accepts my No, then obviously she can't believe very strongly in it. If she's not enthusiastic enough to be willing to fight for it, then why should I buy?"

An objection such as "We can't afford it," or "We already deal with your competitor" may sound like reasons for saying No. But in fact the objection may be a question in disguise, intended to draw you out so the DM can hear how you handle it. Even a flat No may be meant as a subtle, non-committal way of asking you to provide more reasons in support of what you're offering.

In short, the *apparent* objection you hear may *actually* be a way of saying,

- "Give me more information on which to base my decision."

- "Tell me how to handle this objection, because I know I'm going to hear it from others."

- "I'm almost convinced, but I need one more reason to justify my saying yes."

- "Give me a little more proof that your product really will fill my needs."

By the same token, just as objections are often a sign of interest, what sounds like a question may in fact be an objection in disguise. For example, a customer who asks, *"Can your product do . . .?"* may in effect be objecting, *"I think your competitor's product is better, because it can do this. I'm asking the question to give you a chance to prove my assumption wrong."*

Chapter 21: Determining What Is Behind the Question or Objection

People new to selling are sometimes tempted to ignore customer objections, or to try to sweep them under the rug with some sort of quick response, as if getting them out of sight will somehow also get them out of the Decision Maker's mind.

But that's a mistake. You may be able to change the subject away from the Decision Maker's concerns, but the concerns will still be there, and probably stronger than ever because you seemed to be unwilling or unable to deal with them. In this Chapter we look at a better way of responding to the Decision Maker's objections.

The Five-Step Process for responding to objections and questions

There are some questions and objections that are so easy that you can respond to them quickly and directly, and move on.

For our meaning here, that kind of "easy" question or objection is in an area in which your product or service is strong, or that raise issues that you can handle quickly without raising secondary concerns. For example, if the objection relates to a misunderstanding on price that you can set right by pointing to a catalog, do that and move on:

"The answer is yes, we do guarantee our installations for three years, the longest in the industry, according to this survey in

Industry Times which I'll leave with you. Now, moving on to the issue of . . ."

In handling more difficult objections and questions, it's helpful to work systematically through a Five-Step process:

1. *Probe*: basically, you get the DM talking about why he is hesitating; then you,

2. *Listen well to this response.* You may figure you already know the core of the objection, but this person may have a different slant. Listen, hear them through. Don't be too quick in cutting them off to throw out your response.

3. *Restate*: that is, you sum up your understanding of the DM's concerns, and ask the DM to confirm whether that is a fair restatement; if it is, then you,

4. *Respond positively* to that concern, showing how your product or service overcomes that concern; and you,

5. *Move on* to another matter, without getting bogged down on this single issue.

We'll examine the first step – *Probe* -- in this chapter, and the how-to of the other steps in the chapter following.

1. PROBE to find the real point of the objection.

And,

2. LISTEN WELL to this response: attune both to what is said and unsaid.

When the DM raises an objection, or says no, you can't afford to assume that you know what's behind it. The reason this customer is saying No is not necessarily the same reason you've been hearing all week from others.

Often enough, the DM will volunteer a reason. That stated reason may or may not be the real reason, but at least it is a start. (Often the Decision Maker himself may not understand what is really behind his hesitation.)

Sometimes, too, when you ask for Buying Action, the DM will respond with a question or comment, instead of giving a clear Yes or No. That may be a stall, to gain thinking time, or it may be setting up an implied condition.

For example, if you ask the DM to buy, and the DM counters by asking whether you provide service in another area, the DM may be signaling interest in buying, but only if you give that service. Therefore, it's important for you to know what's behind the DM's response: just why is the DM asking a question now, instead of responding to your close?

Similarly, if the DM raises a question or objection, hold off responding to it until you are certain you know precisely why this is a concern to this unique individual. Even though you may have heard this general type of objection many times before, the point which this person is making may be subtly different, perhaps because of some special circumstances of which you are not aware.

Suppose, for example, the Decision Maker says, "We can't afford it." An unskilled entrepreneur's first response might be to try to salvage the sale with a quick offer of a discount. But that's grasping at straws, because you don't really know what the DM means: "Can't afford it" may have any of several meanings. In order to respond effectively, you must know which of them is operating here.

"Can't afford it," may mean, "We don't have money left in this year's budget." If that's the case, then there's no point in offering a price discount -- at least not until you have determined exactly what "can't afford it" means to this customer, at this time.

If you go ahead to offer a price break without knowing what's in the customer's mind, you unnecessarily cheapen your product. You give away profit you might have had. In any case, this year's cut-price will be the starting point for next year's negotiations. Yet, even so, the discount may not be what's actually needed to swing the sale now.

Or, "can't afford it" from another Decision Maker might mean "You haven't yet convinced me of the value of your product. You have failed to show me why your product is worth more money than your competitor's." In this case, a price break might help, but probably not as much as pointing out the additional ways in which your product is better than the competition's.

Situations like this show how important it is to PROBE in order to get the Decision Maker talking. The more the DM tells you, the better are your chances of finding the core objection, and hence of arriving at the best response.

Another response you might hear is that your product is "too expensive." But until you probe to find what this DM means by "too expensive," you'll be operating in the dark. When you do probe, you may find that in fact this DM thinks your product is fairly priced, but she meant something else by "too expensive:" it's expensive in the sense that your product, in the form you offer it, costs $12,000, while this DM has a $10,000 limit for purchasing on her own authority. Anything costing over $10,000 needs to be approved by a higher level. So, for this DM, $12,000 is "too expensive" to buy on her own, without a lengthy approval process, but a pair of $6,000 purchases would be no problem.

Once you learn exactly what this DM's "too expensive" means, you can make it possible for her to buy today simply by changing the terms of your offer from the package deal to a proposal for two separate items, each costing less than $10,000.

"Let me think about it"

"I need to think about it before I can sign," is a common DM response. That seems reasonable enough, and you might be inclined to back off now and offer to come back another day. At first glance, that sounds fair, but it's usually a bad idea. The trouble is, "I need to think" is usually an excuse to avoid thinking. It's often used -- consciously or not -- as a procrastination device to avoid making a decision that should be made on the spot.

Treat it as you would any other objection. Begin by PROBING: "Perhaps I can help? Just what aspect is it you need to think more about?" The DM may tell you a specific concern, and you can go on to respond to it.

But, then again, the DM's response may be vague -- usually because he's not really clear himself on just what he does want to think about. In that situation, it's helpful to probe more specifically. To do that, suggest one possible area, as in, "Is it a cost factor you need to think about?"

If the DM says "Yes, cost is something I need to think about," then focus on that as the objection. Probe it in more detail, then handle it as an objection (that is, *Restate, Respond positively, Move on.*).

If the DM says, *"No, it's not cost I need to think about,"* respond by raising another possible concern, such as, *"Then is it a concern about warranty?"* If that's not it, then move on, suggesting one possibility after another until you have exhausted all the reasonable possibilities (not more than four or five).

At that point, after you have worked through these four or five significant possibilities, say something to the effect,

"We've determined that your reason for hesitating now is not cost, not warranty, not delivery schedules, not financing. From my experience, I've found that these are the main concerns that customers have, but none of them apply here. Tell me, Mr. Lewis, is there any real reason not to sign today? Can we go ahead and write up the order now?"

Phantom objections

Sometimes the real concern will be hidden behind one or more "phantom objections." For example, a customer may raise an objection that seems to concern price, but which is actually a cover to disguise the fact that she does not feel a need strong enough to justify buying.

Or "Too expensive" may be this DM's way of saying that you have not yet proven that your product will in fact fill those needs. Thus it may seem too expensive because it's a gamble whether he will get value for his investment.

Sometimes a price objection or other phantom objection is a smokescreen to hide the fact that the person you have been dealing with does not have the level of spending authority he earlier claimed. Now he's embarrassed to admit that he misled you, so hides behind a phantom objection.

Perhaps you can fit within his authority limits by restructuring your deal into segments. If that's not feasible, you can take this person with you as you move up a step or two on the organizational ladder to find the person with actual Decision Making capability.

Incidentally, if you do try to move up the organizational ladder, make an effort to bring the present person with you. Even though they are not in fact the Decision Maker, they still may be a significant "Decision Influencer," and so can help you make the sale. Besides, you don't want to antagonize them by going over their head.

Probing the Prospect's questions to find and address the real concern

You can also greatly increase your sales effectiveness by using the Five-Step approach as you respond to the questions that the DM raises. In the first place, questions are often disguised objections.

Second, by finding what is behind the question, you gain the opportunity to more closely "target," or "customize" your selling message to the particular concerns of this specific prospect. What the DM asks is important, but even more important is Why the DM is asking it.

Suppose the DM asks if your product is available in green. Or asks how soon you can deliver. Or asks whether you can start immediately on a consulting project.

The answer to any of these questions may be "Yes, of course." But don't be too quick to say it. Instead, PROBE to find why the DM asked. Is it a real concern, or just a passing thought, or a way to procrastinate on making the decision?

Thus you could respond, "Why would green be helpful to you?" Or, "How soon would you need delivery?" Or, "In what ways would it be helpful if I could start immediately?"

If the DM answers, "Well, on second thought, I guess it doesn't matter at all," then you can move on and not waste time. But if she says, "Green equipment is part of our corporate image, and we had to turn down your competitor because they didn't have a green model," then you know you have a key selling point, provided you can supply it. (If not, you can probe some more to explore whether it may be worthwhile developing a customized color to clinch the sale).

Besides, skillful probing may lead the DM to express in his own words just how serious the problem is, and what it's costing. Make note of these DM statements so you can echo them back later as "evidence" to help establish the value of your services, or to convince the DM to take action now.

Probing as a way of making your response seem more valuable

By delaying your answer to probe the reason behind the question, you can target your response. You can also "condition" your response, which may make it seem more valuable.

By pausing to PROBE why that question is important, you project the impression of attaching a condition to your response, which may have the psychological effect of giving greater value to your agreement. Though you can say, "Yes, from what you tell me, I can see why you need this help immediately. I'll find a way to arrange my schedule so I can begin on it tomorrow." Or, "Yes, I can see why green is obviously important to you. I can arrange to have the model available for you in green."

When the Prospect offers shifting reasons

Sometimes, when you probe the prospect's questions or objections, you get a different response with each probe you ask, one after the other. As soon as you deal with one, another comes. Shifting reasons or shifting objections usually means that you have not gotten to the core concern. Keep probing. You might even deal directly with it, saying,

- *"You've raised several different reasons why you're hesitating in buying. From my experience, that usually means there's an even deeper reason. Sometimes the person may not even be consciously aware of just what that deeper concern is. Can we talk about that?"*

- *Or, "What, ultimately, is holding you back from signing today?"*

The simplest probe

The point of probing is to get the DM talking, so you can find out what is preventing the sale from taking place. You can turn that situation around and use it as your probe:

- *"Tell me: what would it take to make this sale happen?"*

- *Or, "Well, then, what do you think your boss would approve?"*

-

Chapter 22: Restating, Responding, and Moving on From Objections

In the previous chapter, we examined the basic approaches for responding to the objections and questions raised by prospects.

With easy questions and objections, respond directly and quickly, then move on. (Easy objections are those in which your product is strong, and in which your response isn't likely to open up other complications.)

For more difficult objections and questions, it's helpful to work through the Five-Step process:

1. *Probe*, to get the DM talking more about his concerns, or why he is hesitating;

2. *Listen well* to the response. This "standard" objection may not be what it sounds like at the start.

3. *Restate*: that is, sum up your understanding of the DM's concerns, and ask the DM to confirm if that fairly restates his position; if so, then you,

4. *Respond positively* to that concern, showing how your product or service overcomes it; and you,

5. *Move on* to another matter; don't let the call bog down on this single issue.

In the previous chapter, we looked at the first of those steps:

1. PROBE. Now we examine the how-to of the four remaining steps.

2. LISTEN WELL to the Prospect's response.

Hear her out even though you are 99% sure you know where this is going. Also "listen through" to any deeper concerns: "too expensive" may mean only that it's more than this month's budget will allow, but perhaps could be fitted into next month's or next year's pot.

3. RESTATE the concern as you understand it.

In this *Restate* phase, your overall objective is to,

- narrow the issue as much as possible, so that you have a clear, manageable target to respond to; and to,

- put that specific concern in context, so the DM can see that, at worst, it is only a minor issue.

In *restating*, sum up your understanding of the core of the DM's question or objection. Try to boil it down into a sentence or two.

As you *restate*, it usually helps to rephrase the concern in the form of a question, as questions tend to be clear and succinct. For example, you might say, "Let me make sure I understand your concern. You find the new warranty program that Competitor X has introduced to be a very important factor in the decision to buy, and I think the question you're implying is whether my company would be willing to match it? Is that a fair understanding of your concern?"

Restating, particularly in question form, may seem unnecessary effort, but it generally more than pays off. First, the paraphrase forces both you and the prospect to attend more closely to what was actually said, and actually meant. That kind of close attention probably won't happen if you merely parrot back the DM's words.

Second, as you rephrase the objection, you may be able to "disarm" it. For example, if the customer objects that it's "too expensive," your restatement question can be, "Let me make sure I understand the point you're making: Are you suggesting that the product seems too costly in relation to the benefits it brings?"

If the customer agrees, "Yes, that is what I meant," then you have created an opening to review the value of your proposal, showing how the dollar costs are outweighed by the benefits.

Alternately, the DM may respond that you haven't quite understood his point: "No, what I meant was that it seems too expensive in comparison with your competition." From that point, you can move in any of several routes. For one approach, you might try to *Restate* your understanding again, refining it.

For a second approach, you can recycle back and *Probe* some more to get a sense of which competitors are most important to the DM, or of precisely how the DM is measuring the cost of those competing products. If you do that, then *Probe* also to find whether that method actually compares oranges with oranges. For example, are they looking only at out-of-pocket expenses, and perhaps overlooking the combined effect of both direct and indirect factors?

Another example: Suppose the Decision Maker says, "I've heard through the grapevine that your products don't hold up well under steady use."

You could rephrase this -- and at the same time disarm it -- by saying, "Your underlying concern, as I understand it, is this: Does my company offer a solid warranty, and do we have service people who can give you immediate assistance if anything should happen to our units? The answer to both is very definitely yes."

As you *Restate*, make it clear to the DM what you are doing, and why. Here are some helpful "signal" phrases to put your *Restating* in context, but add others to the list that feel comfortable to you.

- "Let me make sure I understand your concern: is it that . . . ?"

- "What I'm understanding from your question is that . . ."

- "So that we're both in accord, what I'm hearing from you is that . . ."

If appropriate, you can also Restate not just the actual words used, but the impression you pick up: "What *I'm* sensing is that you tend to feel ____"

4. RESPOND POSITIVELY to that concern.

You might think that between your *Probing* and *Restating* you would be spending too much time before even getting into dealing with the objection itself. In fact, it normally shouldn't take that long to clarify the customer's point. In any case, it's worth the time, as by clarifying the issue and gaining the DM's agreement on what is the precise concern, you gain the advantage of a clear -- and narrow -- target.

It's a lost cause trying to handle a vague, open-ended objection such as, "Your product is too expensive" because that is so broad that you can't really get a handle on it. Does this customer's "too expensive" mean that it costs more than your competition? That it doesn't seem worth the money? That she doesn't have the money? Or is "too expensive" just a negotiating ploy to get you to offer a discount?

The more precisely-focused the DM's concern is, the more specific you can be in your response. That's where first *Probing*, then *Restating* to further define the real issue proves helpful. If you can narrow "too expensive: to something more manageable, like, "Your product costs 10% more than a comparable item from another vendor," or "It costs $1,000 more than my purchasing authorization allows," then you can *Respond Positively* to this narrow concern.

Once you have a clear idea of what the customer's core concern really is, respond to it directly. Deal with the concern fairly, but don't get bogged down. Give a clear response, deal with the objection, then move on.

Responding Positively

However, as you Respond to the prospect's questions or objections, it's important that your response be Positive. It's a mistake to respond in a defensive way, projecting the sense that, "Well, there is a problem with my product, and there's not much I can do about it, but maybe you'll buy anyway." (Even if the words weren't that defensive, one's voice tone and non-verbal communications might have the effect.)

To develop the habit of Responding Positively, first do your homework. Anticipate the kinds of objections that might be raised, and develop clear, succinct responses. If your product is good, be prepared to explain how it is good in this area. If it does have a weakness in this particular area, be able to put that weakness into perspective against all of the things it does well.

Second, pay attention to the subtle messages you project by your expectations and mannerisms as you respond. When a question or objection is raised, answer it with the positive assumption that the DM will easily accept your response. Develop the mindset that your product is so basically sound that any objection, product criticism, or question can be raising only a minor point that you can deal with easily and then move on.

Still another aspect of Responding Positively is to become aware of the subtle signals you project, through your voice tone, body language, facial expression, and the energy and enthusiasm the DM picks up around you. These are just habits, and with awareness of what they are, plus some effort, you can change.

Here's how: "Observe" yourself when you are "in flow," and isolate the tones and mannerisms that come naturally to you then. Define what they are, and even try to describe them on paper. Then make a conscious effort to repeat these mannerisms at a time when you don't naturally feel confident. (True, it's acting, at least at first. Then the new, more positive patterns will become your normal way.)

Moving on

Normally the best way to *Move On* after *Responding Positively* to the objection or question is to ask for a "buying commitment." Proceed on the assumption that your response to the objection cleared up any lingering doubts. Therefore, it's only logical for you to ask for the order as soon as you have dealt with the objection.

Thus if the DM agrees that you have satisfied his concern, you might respond, "Excellent. I can schedule you for installation early next week. Will that be soon enough?"

Don't be compulsive about working through every point you had planned to cover. If the DM is ready to buy now, give her the opportunity. Don't talk so much that you keep her from saying Yes. Respond to the concern without any excess words, then ask for the order.

There's always a risk of talking yourself out of sales by saying too much, particularly if you manage to blow a minor issue into a major block by responding to it at great length. It may have been only a passing thought to the DM, and you don't want to dignify it by paying it too much respect. Give a brief to-the-point response, then move on.

Knowing when it's okay to move on from an objection

How to know whether you have dealt adequately with the objection? First, be sensitive to the DM's signals, verbal and non-verbal. (For some ideas on this, see Chapter 29: Sending and Receiving Non-Verbal Messages in the Sales Situation.)

Second, test your response by asking the customer a variation of, "Does that answer your question?"

The DM's response then gives you the feedback you need: if you have not dealt adequately with the concern, she will say no -- or at least hesitate in signing. Treat that hesitation as an objection, and repeat the cycle of *Probe, Restate, Respond Positively,* backing up to cover the points you skipped over. *Move On,* usually by closing for the sale or other buying action.

The object of the exercise is to get the order, NOT to give a comprehensive sales presentation. The presentation is only a means to an end.

Questions as buying signals

Sometimes, when you look through a prospect's question, or even what appears to be an objection, you find that they are subconsciously signaling their readiness to buy.

For example, you may encounter the question, "How soon could you install?" Or you could run up against the apparent objection, "It just won't do us any good. It's too close to our busy season to take a chance on something new."

Very possibly, both the question and the objection are signaling a message to the effect, "I'm interested in buying, but can you get it up and running quickly, without any bugs or glitches? It's high season coming up, and I can't afford any down-time."

As a sales person, it's tempting to respond immediately to the concern as it is expressed: "Sure, we can help, even though your season is under way." But that can lock you into a dead end.

It's better to Probe before trying to deal with the concern. If the DM's question is, "How soon can you begin?" Probe by asking, "How soon do you need it?" For one thing, that forces the prospect to focus what probably had been just a final vague concern before signing the order.

Similarly, to the objection, "You've got a good product, but we can't think of buying now, because it's too close to our busy season to try something new," PROBE to define the specific concerns, using questions such as, "When does you busy season begin?" and "In what specific ways would you think this new approach could affect the work now? As you push the prospect to be specific, you'll likely encounter one of two effects:

- you will come up with a tangible concern that you can deal with; or,

- the DM will in effect admit that the question/objection was a disguised buying signal: they were all set to buy, provided you could dissolve this last vague doubt.

▪

Chapter 23: Responding To "Early" Objections and Concerns

Objections, concerns, and questions are normal parts of life in selling, so don't back away when you encounter them. The key is to listen well to what the client is really saying, respond in a positive way, then move on.

Refresher: The Five-Step Process for responding to questions and objections

Recall the basic Five-Step process for responding to questions and objections:

1. PROBE to find the real point of the objection.

2. LISTEN WELL to what this unique Prospect is saying; don't cut in.

3. RESTATE the concern as you understand it, normally in question form. (Note: in some cases, particularly if the prospect seems hurried or distracted, it may be necessary to skip the RESTATE step.)

4. RESPOND in a POSITIVE way to the concern as you now understand it.

5. MOVE ON without getting bogged down. Generally, the best way of moving on is to ask the DM to take some form of buying action.

In this chapter, we'll be building from that basic framework by looking at some of the specific objections which you're likely to encounter early in your contacts with either the Screen or DM. (You may encounter these either in your initial phone conversation with the DM, or at the start of the face-to-face meeting.)

1. "You'd only be wasting your time."

As in dealing with any objection, use the Four-Step process. Probe to find why the DM believes you'd be wasting your time. She may be merely trying to scare you off. Then again, she may be raising a serious concern, such as:

She is not the appropriate Decision Maker, as she lacks Authority, Need, or Dollars. Or you have mistaken the role of this department, and she has no involvement at all in buying the kind of services you provide.

She has no money to spend, perhaps because of temporary cash flow problems, or because this is the wrong time in the budget cycle.

The organization has recently purchased a competitive product.

If these are true, then it may not in fact be worth your while to proceed . . . at least not now. But don't give up too easily, as these may only be "phantom" objections -- the DM's proven excuses for brushing off all sales people. Test the DM's firmness, as in this model:

> ■ *"I realize that your budget is particularly tight this year, but I'm confident that what I have to offer will be worth your investment of time. I'll be happy to meet with you at your convenience. Are mornings or afternoons generally better for you?"*

2. "I'm not interested."

Probe and Restate to confirm why this lack of interest, then Respond Positively, and Move On before you become bogged down on this single issue. In responding positively, you may strengthen your statement of benefits, or cite additional successes with other clients.

Often, your probing will uncover that "not interested" really means "not interested in spending time with sales people." Then you can say,

- *"Frankly, Mr. Jordan, most of the lawyers I meet with are just as reluctant as you to spend time. For a professional person, time is money. But it's precisely because your time is valuable that I'm calling. I mentioned a moment ago that we were able to save Bell and Haupt five hundred dollars a month in secretarial time. What I didn't mention was how much of the lawyers' time was also saved -- in the range of several dozen hours per month. I expect you'd be willing to invest a half-hour now in order to save dozens of hours each month in the future, wouldn't you?"*

- Or, *"I understand how you may feel, Mr. Graham. I certainly wouldn't expect you to be interested until I've explained what we have available, and to discuss the many things it will do for you. That's why I think it'll be very productive for us to meet. Would tomorrow or the next day be better?"*

3. "You're calling the wrong person."

Probe to find why the DM is saying this. It may be that you really have come to the wrong person. Perhaps there are two Mr. Robinsons in the company, and this Robinson has nothing at all to do with your specialty.

More often, "wrong person" will be a case of a senior manager referring you down the chain of command to a subordinate who is more closely involved in the technical details. Thus the DM's response may be phrased as, "My job is to practice law (or run a factory), and I leave decisions about equipment to the office manager."

We address how to deal with this in the following item.

4. "Talk to my subordinate about this."

Keep in mind why you contacted this DM, rather than the subordinate: Because your research led to the conclusion that Authority, Need, and Dollars resided here. Perhaps your information was wrong; perhaps sufficient Authority, Need, and Dollars do rest with the subordinate.

Before moving on, take a moment to check this with your present contact:

> - *"I'd be pleased to meet with Mr. Bates. But tell me: If he finds a need for what I'm offering, is he cleared to sign on his own authority? Does he have his own budget for this type of work?"*

If yes, then it's easy: move on to the subordinate, as in this case Mr. Bates appears to be a Decision Maker with Authority, Need, and Dollars.

But if the present DM is retaining final control over the decision, then do whatever you reasonably can to keep your own direct link back to him. One of the most frustrating situations you can get into as a marketer occurs when you lose control over your sale, and find yourself having to rely on a third-party to carry your sales message.

Remember that the subordinate is someone who has only the power to say No -- or to carry your message as he interprets it. Your chances of making the sale are slim if you permit yourself to be cut out of the communication loop, so that your only access to the real Decision Maker is indirectly through the subordinate.

But you can't openly refuse if the DM tries to pass you down to a subordinate. Instead, ask questions: Probe to find why the DM thinks it best to move your level of contact down lower on the organization chart.

It may be that she is assuming that the subordinate is more appropriate since he is more closely involved in the technical side, and so would have a better sense of the Need for your services.

But without Authority or Dollars, the subordinate can be only a "Decision Influencer." Decision Influencers with direct, hands-on awareness of the needs are good to have along as members of the team. But for you to be able to conclude the sale successfully, you must have continuing access to the Decision Maker who controls Authority and Dollars in this matter.

Here's a model for making that point and making the case for this DM to remain personally and directly involved:

- *"Very frankly, Ms. Haynes, the reason I'm calling on you is because we've found that senior executives in your position tend to be more in tune with the overall needs of the company. Their broader perspective enables them to see how this work can provide a broad, cross-functional impact in several departments. While I agree that Mr. Kraft should be present, I also strongly suggest that you remain personally involved, as well."*

When you put it in this context, the DM will likely agree. That gives you access on a continuing basis. But if the DM won't agree to that, push for at least final access back to the DM, so it is you, and not the subordinate, who comes back to the DM to summarize the findings and make the recommendations.

> ▪ *"If Mr. Kraft and I make any significant findings, I would like clearance to come back to you directly, so we can review our progress, and discuss any recommendations that I may find appropriate. Is that agreeable with you? Could we set a tentative time for this follow-on meeting with you? Perhaps two weeks from today?"*

By gaining this kind of commitment from the DM at the start, before you move down the line, you safeguard yourself in a number of ways:

First, you test whether this referral downward is just a way of getting rid of you. By pushing for access back to the DM, you force the issue. If the DM is hiding behind a subordinate because he can't say no, better to find that out now, before you've wasted time and energy on a lost cause.

Further, by retaining your own channel back to the senior person, you gain "clout" with the subordinate. That subordinate will be far less likely to brush you off or to put you at the bottom of their priority list if he knows you will be reporting directly back to the DM.

Keep this channel to the DM open as the work progresses by occasional brief phone calls or letters that both keep him informed, and remind him of the commitment. For example, it may be appropriate to "copy in" the senior person as memos or written findings are developed. (But don't overwhelm the DM in trivia.)

By keeping that continuing channel active, you'll find it easier to re-establish full contact when you are ready to make a demonstration of the product, or to present a written proposal.

If the Prospect won't agree to your continuing direct contact

Don't assume you know the real reason. Probe to tap in on the DM's thinking. Perhaps, without saying so explicitly, the DM is implicitly delegating full buying power to the subordinate. But don't take this delegation for granted. Test it by asking something on the order of,

- *"If Ms. Rigsbee finds our product useful, what will be the purchasing procedure? Will she be able to sign off on her own authority?"*

If the answer is yes, then move on to Ms. Rigsbee. If not, try again to set up at least a tentative time to make your presentation to this DM after your work with Ms. Rigsbee has finished.

- *"I'll phone Ms. Rigsbee for an appointment as soon as I leave your office. After she has had the chance to see my product, I'd like the opportunity to come back with her as we report our findings to you. Can we set a tentative time to meet with you now? Perhaps two weeks from today -- would that be convenient?"*

If the DM still says No -- both to giving a firm commitment to meet with you later, and to delegating purchasing power to the subordinate -- then better give some serious thought to whether it's likely to prove worth your while to proceed any further.

A Decision Maker's unwillingness to commit to a follow-up meeting with you usually means one of three things, none of them promising. He may be indicating he's just not very interested in your product or service. Or he may be implicitly admitting that he's afraid to make the decision, and would rather pass the responsibility on to the subordinate -- though still keeping control of the Authority and Dollars. Or, he is implicitly admitting that he doesn't want to say No to your face, and is hoping that either you take the hint and go away, or that the subordinate will do the dirty work for him.

None of these are positive signs that your investment of time and effort in meeting with the subordinate will pay off for you.

So, given that situation, should you go ahead anyway and make your pitch to the subordinate, in the hope that he'll do a good job of carrying your message to the DM that you can? Of course there is always hope, but the odds of that are so slim that rarely will it be worth your while. No one else can do half the sales job that you can, so why waste your time? It's probably better to use that time finding a better prospect.

5. "I'm too busy."

Probe to find what's really behind this "too busy." Perhaps what the DM really means is that she is temporarily pressed for time. If so, respond,

> ▪ *"I recognize that I may have caught you at a very hectic time. Perhaps it would be more convenient if I called you back. Perhaps the middle of next week, or would two weeks be better?"*

Offering the alternate choice here is essential; otherwise the DM would likely say, "I'll give you a call as soon as things settle down." Odds on, that call will never come. Never let control over timing of call-backs slip out of your hands.

On the other hand, perhaps the DM is permanently overwhelmed by an unending work-flow. This gives you a superb opening if what you're selling offers a way of easing that burden:

- *"I appreciate that you are busy. Most successful executives are extremely busy. In fact, it's specifically to help you ease some of this pressure that I want to meet with you. I can show you how you can free yourself from routine tasks that are eating up your productive work time. I'm asking you to invest a half-hour of your time now in order to save many times that in the longer term. That makes a lot of sense, don't you think?"*

6. "Are you trying to sell me something?"

This is a bluff used to scare away weak sales people. Don't be put off. There's nothing illegal or immoral about trying to make a sale.

But the question does put you in a bind. You can't very well deny that you are trying to make a sale, when in fact that is precisely why you are calling. One good way of countering the question is,

- *"Frankly, it would be very premature to propose a sale at this time. What I first recommend is that we meet personally and discuss your present situation, and how our capabilities may benefit your organization."*

- Or, *"Yes, I am trying to sell you something. I'm trying to sell you increased profitability."*

Note the unexpected effect here, as you propose to sell not a "thing," but rather a result. Who could reasonably refuse to talk about a way of increasing profits? Or of reducing costs or overhead?

7. "Tell me what you have over the phone. Tell me how much it costs."

Since the Decision Maker can't sign the order over the phone, you obviously can't make the sale. But you can lose it if the DM hears just enough to decide not to meet with you.

The request puts you in a bind. Clearly, you can't directly refuse to talk, as the DM in turn would refuse to meet. Here are a couple of models for finessing it:

- *"Mr. Welch, we're in the business of solving problems for our clients, rather than pushing hardware. Until I've met with you, and discussed your interests and needs, I have no way of knowing what we may recommend, nor what it might cost."*

- Or, *"We're a consulting firm, and most of our recommendations involve the use of data processing equipment, but in a variety of contexts. I would need to see you and discuss your needs before I can be more precise."*

8. "Send me some information on this in the mail. Then we'll talk."

Some Decision Makers prefer to read first before meeting with sales people, in the belief that will make the face-to-face discussion more productive. That's understandable from their point of view.

But keep in mind that you are ultimately selling not products or services, but rather the solutions to problems. It's all but impossible for a brochure to make that point as clearly as you. Brochures can't ask the questions that open fresh possibilities.

Your brochure can only help the DM see what the product (or service) IS; few brochures are as able as you to help him see what the product CAN DO.

- *"I understand your position, Mr. Thompson, and it is possible for me to mail you a brochure. But the services we offer are targeted to the clients' specific needs, so I believe it would be more effective if we were to meet in person. This would give me the chance to analyze your areas of specific need. When we meet, I can leave you a brochure. More importantly, I can provide you some additional ideas targeted to your specific interests."*

Then add, without pausing for his reply, "I can drop off the brochure and meet with you on Tuesday morning or Thursday right after lunch. Which would be more convenient?"

- Or, *"Checking my calendar, I see I'll be in your area on Tuesday afternoon. If we can meet for a few minutes then, I'll drop the brochure off personally. That will be faster than the mail, and I'll be able to answer any questions that you may have."*

If the DM's response remains, "Send it first," don't close the door by pushing too hard. Agree to mail what she requests, but make it clear that you will be following it up soon:

- *"I'll be happy to send the information today, then check back with you later in the week, after you've had a chance to look it over."*

It's crucial to make clear from the start that you will be following up on the material you mail. Some people use "send literature" as a way of brushing off sales people.

By making it clear from the start that you will be actively following up soon, you sort out those who are genuinely interested from those who are interested only in getting rid of you. You don't want to turn off anyone, yet there is no point in wasting postage because the supposed Decision Maker can't make a decision.

9. "We already tried something like your product, and we're just not interested."

Probe to find what that "similar" product was, as well as the precise reasons why they decided against it.

Once you know the reasons, treat them as objections, RESTATING and RESPONDING POSITIVELY to each point. Show how your product is either totally different than the other product, or how it avoids the difficulties they encountered previously.

When you Probe regarding that other time they tried something, you may find that the DM's responses are vague. It may be that he does not have a clear memory of just what went wrong before. Or it may be that he is throwing out "already tried it" as a way of shooing you off.

If the DM has no clear answers when you ask why the previous trial was unsatisfactory, take a further step and ask leading questions covering the most likely reasons, then rebut them:

You might ask, "Was it cost that put you off (the competing product)?"

The DM might answer, "You bet. It was just too expensive."

Respond, "Then you'll be interested to know that our new Model Ten costs 30% less, and typically pays for itself within the first year, through increased productivity."

If you get a series of objections, one after another

Probe each of these objections. But if you keep getting a new objection as soon as you resolve the last, something is wrong. A customer might have two or three, or occasionally even five objections or concerns. To get more than that indicates that something deeper is going on.

You can address the issue directly:

- *"We've discussed a number of your concerns, and I think I've dealt satisfactorily with each of them. But when I encounter this many objections, that's usually a signal that there's a deeper concern operating. Can you help me with what that might be?"*

That may spur the DM to open up and raise the deeper issue. But sometimes the string of objections are used to disguise something that he's perhaps embarrassed to talk about: it could be that, despite what he said earlier, he doesn't have the Authority, Need, or Dollars he claimed.

Or maybe there has been a reshuffling in the organization, and his position has suddenly become insecure, and he doesn't feel free to buy anything, yet doesn't want to talk about it.

Summary

In this chapter we focused on responding to "early" objections -- ones that you will generally hear early in the call, even as early as when you phone for an appointment.

The basic framework for dealing with objections is Probe, Listen well, Restate, Respond Positively, then Move On. (Though each step is important, don't be compulsive about the process: for example, if the Decision Maker is impatient, you might cut the Restate step to move things on more in keeping with his tempo.)

Specific early objections to be prepared for are:

1. "You'd only be wasting your time."

2. "I'm not interested."

3. "You're calling the wrong person."

4. "Talk to my subordinate about this."

5. "I'm too busy."

6. "Are you trying to sell me something?"

7. "Tell me what you have over the phone. Tell me how much it costs."

8. "Send me some information by mail. Then we'll talk."

9. "We already tried something like your product, and we're just not interested."

Chapter 24: Handling "Core" Objections

In Chapter 22, we examined the basic model for reacting to objections and difficult questions: *Probe, Listen well, Restate, Respond Positively, Move On.*

Then in Chapter 23 we focused on ways of responding to specific "early" objections -- the kind of roadblocks the Decision Maker or Screen may throw up to avoid meeting with you.

In this Chapter, we shift to methods of dealing with "late" or "core" objections. These are the objections or hesitations that focus on the heart of the matter: That is, on the fundamental question of whether or not the DM will buy.

Though you can encounter these core objections at any time during the sales process, they most commonly arise after you have asked the DM to buy, or to make some other kind of buying commitment.

Though here we discuss specific strategies for coping with the objections, keep in mind that your response should always be within that overall Five-Step response framework: *Probe, Listen well, Restate, Respond Positively, Move On.*

The wording the DM uses in expressing the core objection will vary. Sometimes the objection is expressed more by non-verbal indicators than by the words used. In the items following, you'll find some of these indicators, but be open to other cues that you encounter.

1. The customer's sense of need for what you offer is not strong enough to motivate her to sign the order.

Indicators: No apparent interest. Or. only lukewarm enthusiasm, expressed in phrases such as, "Well, I don't know," or, "Maybe later, but right now we have more pressing needs."

Low enthusiasm may also be expressed by non-verbal signals, such as minimal eye contact, low energy in the voice, apparent boredom or distraction, slumping back in the chair, or general diffidence in manner.

Other indicators include absence of any questions or comments, minimal or indifferent response to the questions you ask, and a general "ho-hum, so-what" demeanor.

Remedy: Use the Five-Step process for defining the real objection -- *Probe, Listen Well, Restate, Respond Positively, Move On.* If a specific objection comes out, react to it.

If no clear problem emerges, recycle back to the "Consultative Selling Wedge" sequence of questions (Chapter 10), and try again to develop or enhance the DM's sense of need for your product. In doing this, you may try to develop the DM's awareness in greater depth of the practical implications of the needs which you already discussed. Alternately, you may look for additional needs.

2. The customer is not convinced that your product offers good value.

Indicators: Phrases such as, "I don't think we can justify the cost," or, "Too expensive," or, "I frankly don't think it's worth the money to us."

Remedy: Recycle back to the wedge sequence of selling questions (Chapter 10) to further develop the Decision Maker's awareness of the various types of value offered by your product or service as it would help this specific organization.

3. Although the DM recognizes that a need does exist, she is not convinced that what you offer can in fact fill that need.

Indicators: Phrases such as, "It's an attractive package, but I'm not sure it can do the job for us," or, "How can I be sure it'll do what you say?"

Other indicators include a series of technical questions that focus on specific details of what you propose. These signal that the prospect is testing whether your product has the capability of fulfilling all you promise.

Remedy: Use the Five-Step process for finding the specific area of doubt – *Probe, Listen well, Restate, Respond Positively, Move On.* Then offer a proof source that is appropriate to that concern.

What type of proof source to use will vary both with the circumstances and the kinds of concerns the DM is expressing:

One proof source might be a demonstration of your product in action to show how it works, or how it will fill the specific need.

Or you may demonstrate sample products.

Or the appropriate proof source might be a written proposal showing how you arrived at the cost savings you promise.

References from similar organizations that have successfully used your product or services to solve related needs can also serve as very effective proof sources.

Part Seven provides guidance on the major kinds of proof sources available, and when and how to use them.

4. Although the DM recognizes that significant needs exist, he is not convinced that yours is the best available way of filling those needs.

Indicators: Phrases such as, "In my mind, Microsoft has always been the standard of the marketplace, and I'm reluctant to change." Or, "We've been looking at the Remco Whizzer. How does your product differ from that?"

Additionally, a series of technical questions may indicate that the customer is comparing your product with that of others she has studied -- which means that they are exploring the idea of buying a product like yours. So apparently the need is clear to the DM, and what is now at issue is whether your product is the one that can best and most cost-effectively fill that Need.

Remedy: Subtly PROBE to find which of your competitors are also on the DM's short list, and why. That information gives you some clues on what capabilities are of particular interest.

Target your responses accordingly: Restate your understanding. RESPOND POSITIVELY by detailing the specific ways in which your product is better than the competing product the DM is most interested in.

As you Respond Positively, avoid going to either extreme, of speaking only in generalities, without offering any evidence to back up what you say, or of becoming bogged down in technical details, without establishing the overall context.

In presenting your proof, set the context with a general statement, then offer back-up detail to prove your general statement. Here's a model:

"The GEM 4000 provides a 30% higher output than the Remco Whizzer. For example, in an independent lab study comparing the two units, the GEM 4000 turned out an average of 130 widgets per hour over an eight-hour span, while the Remco Whizzer, which advertises 100 per hour, actually averaged only 80 per hour. In addition, the Whizzer broke down three times during the test period."

5. The DM seems both to recognize the need and to like your product, but claims that no money is available.

Lack of money or insufficient cash flow can be real concerns. But "no dough" is often used as a phantom objection either to hide a deeper concern, or to brush you off. Use the Five-Step process (Probe, Listen well, Restate, Respond Positively, Move On) to determine which it is here. Useful questions in probing this issue include:

- *"Would it change things if we could arrange a lease in order to reduce the front-end payment?"*

- *Or, "We do have an economy model, which I'd be pleased to demonstrate at your convenience. Perhaps tomorrow at this same time?"*

If nothing else seems to break through, you might try this: "Just suppose for the moment that it were possible for me to cut the price in half -- would you buy in that case?" (This is useful as a way of probing a suspected phantom objection. But make clear from the start that this is a "just suppose." You don't want the DM to think that you are actually offering this large a reduction.)

6. The Prospect says in effect, "I like it. But not now."

There are situations when the present is truly not a good time to buy. But more frequently, "Not now" is a phantom objection that you need to dissolve in order to find what's really behind the DM's reluctance.

In probing here, ask questions on the order of,

- *"We've explored the facts, and found that this improvement can save your company over $2,000 per month. With savings like this possible, how can you hesitate when each passing month means another $2,000 slipping away?"*

There may be genuine reasons why no purchasing decision can be made at this time, such as low cash flow, or the fact that you have arrived at the wrong phase of the annual purchasing cycle. If that's the case, at least keep the door open to future business by agreeing on a call-back date.

7. The "Final" Objection.

Sometimes you'll find that as soon as you handle one question or objection, the prospect raises another. A few objections are to be expected, but an endless stream of them usually means that the DM is dancing away. Here's a way of taking one of those objections and making it the DM's final objection.

Basically you use a modified form of the Five-Step process for responding to objections: Probe to find the core concern, then Restate that concern in your own words "so you can better understand it."

As you Restate this objection, make a point of agreeing with the DM on the importance of that objection. You might even reinforce the significance of the point, by saying something on the order of, "I can understand the importance of this concern. I agree that the equipment would not be of much value to you unless it could (whatever is relevant to your product)."

Then go on to say, "In fact, that's probably the only thing standing between us, isn't it? If my equipment could do (whatever the objection relates to) then you would probably buy -- right?" The DM will usually agree.

Next, carry the point further by asking the DM to explain the point of his concern. "Just to clarify my thinking, why is this particular capability so important to you?"

Your point here is to determine if this is the real, most basic objection. You will likely get one of three kinds of responses:

He will explain why this issue is of particular importance to him. In this case, he becomes committed to the position. Respond to it using the Five-Step process, and conclude by asking for the order. It's only natural for you to ask for the order, since the DM has already admitted that he would buy if you can show that your product can overcome the difficulty.

Or, while he is trying to explain the importance of his concern he will touch on the real objection. He may not even have been consciously aware of it until that point, so listen carefully both to what is said and to what is implied, so you can spot this buried objection. Then use the Five-Step process for responding to that objection.

Or, in the course of explaining why it is important to him, he will realize that the concern sounds silly when put into words, and drop the point. Move On, generally by closing for the order or other kind of buying action.

Keeping yourself and your product in the Prospect's mind
If wait you must, look for ways of reminding the DM over the succeeding weeks and months that you still exist and want the business.

For example, in the course of your travels you may come upon a news clipping relevant to the DM's business or industry -- particularly from an out-of-town publication that he may not have seen. Send it, along with your business card and a short note: "For Your Information," or, "Thought you might find this of interest."

Also, be sure to send the DM a copy of your newest brochure or catalog when it comes off the press, along with a short personal note. The note need not be long, just something on the order of, *"Here's our new brochure. As you will notice, we have introduced several new features since we talked in October. I recall your mentioning then that planning for your upcoming fiscal year begins in June, and I will be in contact with you then."*

Summary

The basic framework for dealing with objections and tough questions is *Probe, Listen well, Restate, Respond Positively, Move On.* Keep that in mind as the basic model. Using that framework as a base, along with the specific responses addressed in this chapter, be prepared for common "core" objections, such as these:

1. The customer's sense of need for what you offer is not strong enough to motivate her to sign.

2. The customer is not convinced that the product is a good value for the money.

3. Although the customer recognizes that a need does exist, she is not convinced that what you offer can truly fill that need.

4. The DM recognizes that the need exists, but is not convinced that you are offering the best possible solution.

5. The DM seems to be in favor of what you offer, but claims that no money is available.

6. The customer says in effect, "I like it. But I don't want to buy now."

7 The "final" objection.

Chapter 25:   Dealing with Other Problems with the Decision Maker

Although the "other problems" that we'll be looking at in this Chapter are not objections in the normal sense of the word, the same Five-Step process (Probe, Listen Well, Restate, Respond Positively, then Move on) helps in cutting to the core of the difficulty.

1. You hear an endless string of objections.

Indicators: It seems that as soon as you demolish one objection the prospect raises another, and then another. A string of relatively insignificant objections, thrown out one after the other, usually signals that there is a deeper underlying problem that you have not dealt with.

Before you can make any progress you MUST break out of the pattern of reacting to these one-by-one, and PROBE to the core of the root difficulty. (Often, the DM herself is not consciously aware of just what that ultimate difficulty is, and has only a vague feeling of unease about the situation.)

Sometimes, the customer may throw up this string of objections because she's embarrassed to admit that she doesn't have as much buying authority as she had claimed. Or that the rules of the game in the organization have changed since you first talked, so her authority has been diminished.

Or it may be that although she does have Authority, Need, and Dollars, she is worried about the economic climate over the next few months.

Remedy: How to deal with the string of objections? As ever, Probe, Listen Well, Restate, Respond Positively, then Move On.

But in this case, you'll need to be flexible and creative in how you probe. For example, you could begin by confronting the hesitation head-on, in hopes of unblocking the DM's root concerns:

- *"You're raising a variety of issues, but I sense there's a deeper concern that's troubling you."*

If that doesn't break through, draw on a combination of intuition and experience, and say something on the order of, "I sense that behind your hesitation may be some concerns about which way the economy is heading. Could that be at the core of it?"

If the customer concedes that Yes, what you suggest is indeed the root cause, Then Respond Positively to it. *Do not* slip into a defensive mode.

Thus, if the concern is the economic climate, you could respond by showing how the savings resulting from installing your product will more than pay for the out-of-pocket expense. Thus the purchase would make sense regardless of the direction the economy takes.

2. You realize, after encountering a series of phantom objections, that this person does not in fact have the necessary Authority, Need, or Dollars.

Indicators: You make your presentation and feel interest on the DM's part. But then you encounter a string of weak objections, one after another.

Look through the objections to what is being said underneath. Perhaps the person is ultimately saying, "I can't really make that decision," or "I can't make it alone." Sometimes Decision Makers suddenly find that they don't have as much authority as they assumed they had. Perhaps your proposal surprised them by coming in above their purchasing limit. Or perhaps they picked up on changing political undercurrents in the organization, and realize that it's prudent to get higher-level sign-offs to cover themselves.

Remedy: If you find out fairly late in the sales cycle that your contact really does not have full Authority, Need, or Dollars, you have two main choices:

First choice: You can withdraw from the call at this point, and attempt to re-establish your contact with the organization at a higher level.

But if you leapfrog over your present contact, you may lose a friend whose feelings are hurt that you went over his head. It may turn out that although she's not the Decision Maker, she may be a significant influencer of the final decision. Or you may come back a few months from now, to find that the person you cut around is now sitting in the Decision Maker's chair.

Second choice: It usually works out better to try to move upward to the appropriate level, while taking this person with you. That gives you the chance to make your case directly to the DM, and at the same time gives the present contact an opportunity to gain favorable exposure to a senior manager in a way that he might not otherwise have been able to arrange on his own.

To accomplish this shift, you might say,

- *"I agree with you, and I'd be very pleased to meet with Mr. Jackson. I'd like you to come with me when I make that call. Shall I set up an appointment with Mr. Jackson, or would you prefer to do it for us?"*

If the present contact agrees to set up the appointment with the senior manager, set a time to check back with him to confirm the date. The knowledge that you will be checking back reduces the likelihood of procrastination.

However, if you do try back a couple of times with this contact, and each time find that he has still not made the call, step in and offer to make the call yourself.

Caution: don't delegate the sale

When the sale moves up to a higher level within the organization, make sure that you move up with it.

You can count on your message being garbled if you let someone else try to do your selling for you. No matter how enthusiastic this other person is, the reality is that he does not know your product and its capabilities the way you do. He simply won't be able to handle the senior manager's questions and objections.

Besides, a lower-level manager will tend not to be very aggressive in following through, or in pushing for a Yes decision. After all, naturally enough, his main objective is to keep his job, not to make a sale for you.

3. For some reason, you and the DM seem to grate on each other's nerves.

You may be able to defuse this hostility simply by articulating what you are picking up:

"Mr. Roberts, I sense that for some reason you and I got off on the wrong foot. I don't know why this happened, but I'd like to try and overcome it."

It may well be that the DM's tension has nothing to do with you at all. Perhaps you walked in just after a rough session with his supervisor.

If you can't salvage the situation reasonably quickly, then it may be best to cut your losses and move on . . . either to another prospect organization, or to another person within this present organization.

Sometimes all it takes is to come back and make a fresh start another day.

4. It appears that the DM is displeased with or hostile to your organization, or is concerned about the risks of dealing with a small entrepreneur.

If doubts exist, there's no point in hiding your head in the sand. Probe to find the root cause of the customer's doubts. Bring them out in the open so you can deal with them. Probe, Listen Well, Restate Positively, Respond, Move On.

5. You realize that this individual is psychologically incapable of making a decision.

There's no easy solution to this one. When possible, you can attempt to maneuver the decision to a higher level in the organization by helping the indecisive person find someone to whom he can pass the buck -- perhaps to his boss, or to a committee or task force.

The DM may even be open to delegating the decision downward to a subordinate who is strong enough to step in and fill the vacuum.

6. You discover that the organization actually has no need for what you offer.

If you're certain of this, admit it as soon as you know. This saves both your own and the Decision Maker's valuable time.

Even more importantly, it projects your professionalism. The gesture builds good will and credibility with the customer -- useful currency if you should want to call again in the future when your product or their needs change.

In any case, keep the door open for later call-backs. Leave product literature for their files. Offer to put them on your mailing list for any new product announcements, special offers, and the like.

And, as always, ask for referrals -- people or organizations the DM thinks may have a need for your product.

Summary

Though, strictly speaking, these are neither questions nor objections, these special problems that arise in your relationship with the DM can usually be defused by using the Five-step process: *Probe, Listen Well, Restate, Respond Positively, Move On.*

1. You hear an endless string of objections.

2. You realize, after encountering a series of phantom objections, that this person does not in fact have the necessary Authority, Need or Dollars.

3. For some reason, you and the DM seem to grate on each other's nerves.

4. It appears that the DM is displeased with or hostile to your organization, or is concerned about the risks of dealing with a small entrepreneur.

5. You realize that this individual is psychologically incapable of making a decision.

6. You discover that the organization actually has no need for what you offer.

Acknowledgements

This book could not have been written without the ideas and support provided by consulting clients, master sales people, and friends, particularly, Barry Blum, Mary Casteel, Ray Croft, Frank Dombroski, John Fairs, Paul Foster, Joe Harless, Nick Iuppa, Stephanie Jackson, William F. Jordan, Paul Landauer, Claude Lineberry, Larry Martin, Susan McGaulley, William A. Mulligan, Neil Rackham, Phil Scatterday, Bruce Stanton, Paul Tremlett, Bob Tuomey, and other sales people who shared ideas, and suffered having a silent partner watching them work.

Xerox Corporation, Xerox of Canada, Rank-Xerox, Kodak, GTE/Sylvania, Motorola, and Bank of America sponsored some of the consulting work that provided the background for the approaches in this book.

Other books in my two series:

- **The Small Business Sales How-to Series, and,**
- **Career Savvy People Skills Series**

The books in the two series described here flow from my experience first as a lawyer, then a management consultant working with companies that included Xerox in the United States, Canada and Europe; Kodak; Sylvania; Bank of America; Motorola, and others.

Part of my work involved analyzing the key skills and competencies that make the difference between top-performing managers, sales people and sales managers, then developing training programs, guides, and job-aids to teach these skills to new trainees and those who had been working below their full potential. The books in this series draw from that experience.

See my blog/website at **www.Selling-face-to-face.com** for additional tips and ideas, as well as contributions by other readers.

I hope that *Selling 101: Consultative Selling Skills* has proven helpful to you. If so, then as a favor I'd appreciate your leaving a reader review on the Amazon page. Here's the link directly to the page:

https://www.amazon.com/review/create-review?&asin=0976840669

Thank you,

Michael

Books in the *SMALL BUSINESS SALES HOW-TO SERIES:*

Book #1: 25 SALES HOW-TO TUTORIALS

Small Business Sales How-to
Book #1

25 Sales How-to Tutorials

A Step-by-step Guide for New Entrepreneurs, Self-employed, Career Changers

Michael McGaulley

TUTORIALS is a step-by-step guide for new entrepreneurs, self-employed folks, and career changers. It's built tutorials that you don't just read but go beyond and use as models for developing your own sales messages. It's especially targeted to the needs of career-changers and people going off on their own, or looking for a new job or a new field—such as consultants, free-agents, or independent contractors.

Book #2: SELLING 101: CONSULTATIVE SELLING SKILLS

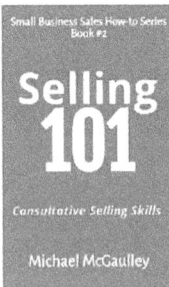

Small Business Sales How-to Series
Book #2

Selling 101

Consultative Selling Skills

Michael McGaulley

SELLING 101 is directed to more experienced salespeople who want access the kind of sales training courses I developed for major marketing firms including Xerox, Kodak, and others.

Book #3: SALES TRAINING WORKSHOP LEADER GUIDE

Small Business Sales How-to
Book #3

Sales Training Workshop Leader Guide

Coordinates
with:

Selling 101

Michael McGaulley

THE *SALES TRAINING WORKSHOP LEADER GUIDE* is the instructor's guide coordinated with the text, *Selling 101: Consultative Selling Skills.*

Who this sales training workshop--leader guide is intended for

Sales managers looking for materials for sales team meetings.

Instructors in new entrepreneur training workshops.

Instructors in community colleges or similar job-training programs

What this sales training workshop - leader guide provides

The 14 Modules in the Workshop Leader Guide track the coverage in **SELLING 101**, linking to specific pages for ease in linking across.

A chart at the start of each Module provides a succinct overview of what that module is about, suggested time to allow, as well as materials and set-up.

The content within the modules guide the instructor or leader through clearly-marked sections, such as

- Overview and set context,

- Lead discussion,

- Explain,

- Pair trainees for one-on-one role plays,

- Conduct whole-group debriefing, and,

231

- Wrap-up and overview the next module.

Pre-class assignments for each module are provided, which the workshop leader can copy and pass out in advance. These guide the trainee on the reading assignment (chapters or sections from the course text, Selling 101), as well as other preparation, such as discussions and role-play exercises to prepare for.

Book #4:   HOW TO DELIVER PROFESSIONAL PRESENTATIONS & DEMONSTRATIONS

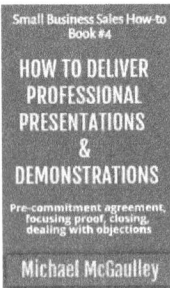

HOW TO DELIVER PROFESSIONAL PRESENTATIONS & DEMONSTRATIONS covers the practical how-to of presenting or demonstrating in front of the prospect, as well as the very important matter of reading (and sending) non-verbal messages. It also addresses the essential point that demonstrations, presentations, proposals, free-trials, discounts and other special deals are "proof sources," given for a specific, defined purpose, agreed-upon in advance with the prospective buyer.

Books in the *CAREER SAVVY PEOPLE SKILLS SERIES:*

Book #1: *AM I ASKING THE RIGHT QUESTIONS?*

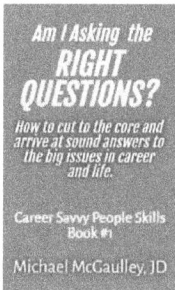

Am I Asking the
RIGHT
QUESTIONS?
How to cut to the core and
arrive at sound answers to
the big issues in career
and life.

Career Savvy People Skills
Book #1

Michael McGaulley, JD

"You've got to stay aware of the games that are being played. You don't have to play the games yourself, but you do need to recognize when they are being played against you."

RIGHT QUESTIONS *provides an array of tools for cutting* to cut to the core and arriving at sound answers to the big issues in career and life.

Book #2: MENTAL PICKPOCKETING

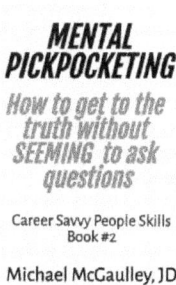

MENTAL
PICKPOCKETING
How to get to the
truth without
SEEMING to ask
questions

Career Savvy People Skills
Book #2

Michael McGaulley, JD

When you ask a question, most people, most of the time, will do their best to tell the truth. But not always.

MENTAL PICKPOCKETING introduces you to an array of methods of getting to the truth without *seeming* to ask questions.

Book #3: *UN-PUZZLING PERSONALITIES*

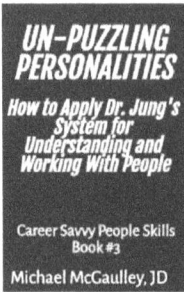

UN-PUZZING PERSONALITIES
PERSONALITIES

How to Apply Dr. Jung's System for Understanding and Working With People

Career Savvy People Skills
Book #3

Michael McGaulley, JD

UN-PUZZING PERSONALITIES is based on a system developed by Carl Jung for understanding and working with individuals, teams, and other groups.

Use it for viewing yourself from fresh perspective, as well as a tool for understanding the different ways others perceive and react to events and communications.

Websites:

SalesTrainingSource.com

MichaelMcGaulley.net

Legal and copyright notices continued from the front of this book

Necessary legal disclaimers, provisos, and such

The contents of this book reflect the author's views acquired through experience in the areas addressed. The author is not engaged in rendering any legal, financial or accounting advice. Business customs, courtesies, and legal implications vary with the context, and with geographic region or country. Accordingly, anyone reading this material should not rely totally on the contents herein, and should seek the advice of others. The author has made his best effort to ensure that this is a helpful and informative manual. The contents are recommendations only, and the author cannot take responsibility for loss or action to any individual or corporation acting, or not acting, as a result of the material presented here.

While the information contained within the pages of this electronic book, other related books and e-books, and the related web-site, is periodically updated, no guarantee is given that the information provided is correct, complete, and/or up-to-date.

The materials contained in this e-book and related website are provided for general information purposes only and do not constitute legal or other professional advice on any subject matter. Neither the author nor publisher accept any responsibility for any loss which may arise from reliance on information contained in this book or related website.

Some links within this e-book or related website may lead to other websites, including those operated and maintained by third parties. The author and publisher of this e-book include these links solely as a convenience to you, and the presence of such a link does not imply a responsibility for the linked site or an endorsement of the linked site, its operator, or its contents.

The publisher and author accept no liability whatsoever for any losses or damages caused or alleged to be caused, directly or indirectly, by utilization of any information contained herein, or obtained from any of the persons or entities herein above.

www.ingramcontent.com/pod-product-compliance
Lightning Source LLC
Chambersburg PA
CBHW060008210326
41520CB00009B/861